STUDY TO BE QUIET

Hearing From God In and Out of Crisis

Timothy Houston

Houston Publishing

DEDICATION

To my Lord and Savior Jesus Christ, this book is the product of time spent alone with you. If I were to write all the wonderful things you have shared with me during our quiet times together, I would have a thousand books just like this one. I love you Jesus.

To my wife Linda, this has been an awesome journey. You are a wonderful wife. I look forward to what our future together holds. I thank God for blessing me with you.

To my children, Anetra, Tinesha, Nicole, Tim Jr., and Tamia, you have always been a source of inspiration for me. It is because of you that I am above all men most richly blessed.

To my pastor, Superintendent Stephen Stallworth and the Greater Grace C.O.G.I.C. church family, thank-you for consistently ministering a fresh new word into my spirit. Greater Grace is my sanctuary.

To the late Pastor Hurley Coleman Sr., and the Coleman Temple C.O.G.I.C. church family, you are my genesis. I am the product of your labor and you will always be able to refer to me as your own. Thank you for allowing me to be your son.

To my mother Levater, and my sisters, Annie, Betty, Joann, and my brothers, J. T., Wilbert, and Silas, I know you are "excited" for me. You have encourgered me throughout my ministry and have allowed me to be your minister. Thank you for your support.

To my sister-in-law Ruby, thank-you for the hours you put into this book. You helped bring it to fruition, and it is a better book because of your input.

To Vanessa Jones, "You have the Power." You gave me the direction I needed to move forward. May God bless you in all your writing endeavors.

To the family of God all over the world, your Heavenly Father is waiting to share wonderful things with you. Enjoy this book. It is for you that I write.

CONTENTS

INTRODUCTION

God's Response to Terrorism

On Sept. 11, 2001, I was sitting in bed when I saw the news. I could not believe what I was hearing. As a minister, my first instinct was to pray. In shock and amazement, I began to pray, then the second plane hit. No more praying, just silence. How could this be? What is going on? The third plane hits. Life leaves out of me. The first building falls. Oh my God! I must be dreaming. I wanted to wake up. The second building falls. I can not take much more. What can I do Lord? How can I help? I felt the hand of God touch me. I began to write. These are the words that I wrote.

Death is an enemy of God. It will be destroyed. *The last enemy that shall be destroyed is death (1 Cor 15:26)*. Death is a tool of the devil. Satan comes to steal, kill, and destroy. He uses people as his instrument of death. He used Pharoh to kill thousands of children in an attempt to kill Moses. *And Pharaoh charged all his people, saying, Every son that is born ye shall cast into the river, and every daughter ye shall save alive (Exodus 1:22)*. He used Herod to kill thousands more children in an attempt to kill Jesus. *Then Herod, when he saw that he was mocked of the wise men, was exceeding wroth, and sent forth, and slew all the children that were in Bethlehem, and in all the coasts thereof, from two years old and under, according to the time which he had diligently enquired of the wise men (Matt 2:16)*.

On Sept. 11, 2001, satan used terrorist to kill thousands in an attempt to kill the spirit of the American people. He did not succeed in the past and he will not succeed today. Killing people won't kill faith, hope, and love. Satan has stolen lives, but he can not steal love. *Fear thou not; for I am with thee: be not dismayed; for I am thy God: I will strengthen thee; yea, I will help thee; yea, I will uphold thee with the right hand of my righteousness (Isaiah 41:10).*

God wants us to live. The Bible says, *"I have come that you may have life, and have it more abundantly (John 10:10)."* He is not the agent of death, satan is. God is the giver of life. He can not give death and life at the same time. He would be at war with himself and his Kingdom could not stand. *According to the word, And if a kingdom be divided against itself, that kingdom cannot stand (Mark 3:24).* We have to know that God is opposed to death, as it is in his word, *And death and hell were cast into the lake of fire (Rev 20:14).* He is opposed to those who would use death to terrorize. They will be cut down. *Fret not thyself because of evil men, neither be thou envious at the wicked; For there shall be no reward to the evil man; the candle of the wicked shall be put out (Proverbs 24:19,20).*

Fret not thyself because of evildoers, neither be thou envious against the workers of iniquity. For they shall soon be cut down like the grass, and wither as the green herb (Psalms 37:1,2).

So many questions, and we need answers. The answers we seek are in God. Study to be Quiet is about learning to hear from God, especially in times of crisis. God wants to talk to you. He can warn us about future attacks. He will give us peace. *Peace I leave with you, my peace I give unto you: not as the world giveth, give I unto you. Let not your heart be troubled, neither let it be afraid (John 14:27).*

For God hath not given us the spirit of fear; but of power, and of love, and of a sound mind (2 Tim 1:7).

America is still one nation under God, and in God we trust. We are strong because we have overcome adversity. We will not bow down. The last enemy to be destroyed is death, and death will be destroyed. I pray this book will help you see the real plan God has for you. *For I know the thoughts that I think toward you, saith the LORD, thoughts of peace, and not of evil, to give you an expected end. Then shall ye call upon me, and ye shall go and pray unto me, and I will hearken unto you (Jeremiah 29:11,12).*

GOD BLESS AMERICA

CHAPTER ONE

HOW IT ALL GOT STARTED

"AND THAT YE STUDY TO BE QUIET"
1 THES 4:11

I know God does instant healing and deliverance. The Bible is clear on that but not all deliverance and cleansing will be instantaneous. Some things require us to spend time alone with God. I know this is a sacrifice, but you are worth the effort. Time alone with God will not only cleanse us of our present "stuff," but will also steer us clear of future traps and snares of the enemy. I personally thank God for every pastor and minister who takes time to pray for those in need. Let us continue to use all the gifts that God has given us to destroy the works of the devil.

God bless you.

Prayer and Meditation

*But his delight is in the law of the Lord; and in his law doth
he meditate day and night. (Ps 1:2)*

There are some definite times in our lives when we
really need to hear from God. I personally experienced one
of those times about six years ago. My life seems to have
exploded right before my eyes. Nothing was familiar. My
thoughts were rushed. My peace was lost, and my joy was
gone. I really needed to hear from my Heavenly Father.
The word of God I received at church was awesome, but
I still needed more. My situation required God's personal
attention. It required step-by-step instruction on how to
put the pieces of my life back together. I knew how to pray,
so I began to pray. The more I prayed, the more frustrated
I became. I was praying, but I was not hearing. I really
wanted to hear God, but I just didn't know how. I heard
God in the past, and I needed to hear from him now.

I was explaining my situation to a friend of mine. She
told me that I needed to meditate on the Lord. I did not
like the sound of that. It sounded like she was asking me
to chant or something. "Not my thing," I told her. I was
always of the opinion that because prayer required you to
meditate they were basically the same things, but I was willing to listen to her. So after a couple of hours of discussion,
reading, and some more discussion, I left the conversation
with the same understanding I went in with. The time on
the phone was not wasted. This conversation started a
desire in me to understand what the Father meant when He
said meditate on his word.

You see, I had the right idea, but the wrong source.
Friends can only give you opinions about prayer and meditating on God's word, but the real truth is in God. Your
source of information about God should be God. All other
sources can only tell you what they think. God will tell you

what he knows. I thought I did not have time to learn how to hear from the Lord. I thought it would take too long. Boy was I wrong! It takes longer to go to the wrong source. It takes longer to operate on opinions.

I did know enough to know that prayer and meditating on the Word were not the same things. Think about it, though football requires you to block, football and blocking are not the same things. Baseball requires you to run, but running and baseball are not the same things. My friend had shown me though prayer required you to meditate, meditating on the Word and prayer are not the same things. Though math may require you to add and subtract, we teach them individually until you thoroughly understand each one separately and then we teach you how to use them together. Prayer and meditating on the Word are not the same thing! Now I could become a student of prayer and a student of being still before the Lord!

How many more people have thought the same thing? How many others were missing out on the wonderfulness of being still before God? I had to see prayer and being still as being separate before I could study them separately. What is meditating on the Word? What is prayer? The following little story shows us why it is important to define what we mean up front.

Getting Vicious

A youth football coach called one of his players to him and said, "I want you to go into the game and I want you to get vicious"! The little lad turned and ran onto the field toward the other players. He gets about halfway to the huddle, and screams back at the coach, " Hey coach, which one is Vicious"! The boy and his coach had a different idea about what it meant to get vicious. You have to be very careful to ensure what you say is not lost in the translation. It is very important for you to define words before you use them. What means one thing to one person can mean something totally different to someone else.

Prayer- an address (as a petition) to God in word or thought.

Meditation- Quiet contemplation or reflection.

If prayer is talking to God, then being still is listening to God. Prayer is the petition; being still gets the answer. When I talk about meditation I am not talking about chanting, I am talking about quietly listening to God. The Bible tells us to "study to be quiet, or in other words study how to be still, or the art of being quiet. God spoke through the psalmist and said *"Be still and know that I am God" Psalms 46:10.* Being still is a quiet reflection on God. When you see the word "meditation" throughout this book, think of it to mean still quiet reflection on God, or listen to God for answers. Now we can get "vicious."

Purpose of this Book

This book can help the minister that is overwhelmed with his work. It can help strengthen the mom that is struggling with the kids, husband and housework. It will comfort the divorcee dealing with life after the demise of his/her marriage, and guide those in search of answers to their problems. This book will help students of all ages learn how to be still so they can receive instructions. This book gives you the tools to find the answers to your problems. It provides the tools for you to know God more and to know his will for you.

There is a special place in my heart for our teens. They are under constant spiritual and emotional attack. They are constantly rushing. They rush out of the house each morning. They rush to school, and they rush to class. The time between class is shorter, but the distance between class is greater. This makes them rush even more. They hurry to lunch, to eat in a hurry. To add to the madness, they rush to football, basketball, or soccar practice, to band and to clubs. Finally, they rush home to chores, homework, television, and to bed. The next day they get up and start all over again. They are emotional time bombs waiting to explode.

We need to teach them how to slow down. Quiet time with their Heavenly Father resets their emotional clock. He empties out their closet of worries and frustrations. He gives them the opportunity to check out themselves before they interact with others. God is the solution to the rage that has been unleashed in our school. Teaching our teens how to slow down also teaches them how to calm down. We all, regardless of age, need God to put order in our lives.

Our lives are out of order and only God can truly order our steps. Daily adjustments from God keep us from drifting off course. The truth of the matter is, when it comes to God, we talk too much. Listen! For he is the God of all knowledge. He knows your will and your ways. He even knows your thoughts. Listen to learn His. He is omniscient, the possessor of all knowledge. Meditate on his words.

This book is the "why" you should meditate on His law. *"Meditate on these things; give yourself entirely to them, that your progress may be evident to all (1Tim 4:15).* Giving yourself entirely to the word of God causes you to progress. This book is part of it, and you're the rest of the equation. Your progress is predicated on your attention being placed on the word of God. You must give yourself. No one else can do it for you. It is more than just reading the Bible.

Reading a book on golf will not make you a good golfer. That requires practice, or should I say perfect practice. Many of us have practiced golf on our own, only to develop bad posture, position, and swing. To be a good golfer you must study the art of golf, and you must practice good golf principles. The more you study the principles and practice them, the better you get. Being quiet is the same way. You have to do it to get better! Like golf, if you rely on practice alone you will develop bad habits such as bad posture, timing and position. These are all the results of not being properly instructed. Study to be quiet. You are worth the time, energy, and effort of studying and putting what you learn into action. This book contains principles that if put into practice, will help you hear from God. Let us begin, your Heavenly Father is waiting for you.

CHAPTER TWO

"SLOW DOWN, YOUR FATHER IS TALKING!"

"BE STILL AND KNOW THAT I AM GOD"
(PSALMS 46:10)

My son ran past me in haste. I attempted to stop him, but all I got was "I got to go Dad, I got to go really bad!" My attempt to slow him down was to no avail. He was in a hurry to find the bathroom. "Wait a minute son!" I shouted as he ran past me in the opposite direction. Too late, he wanted to hear what I had to say, but the situation at that moment was too <u>pressing</u>. Zoom! He made another turn past me. "If you would just be still....," were my words that followed him down yet another corridor. I wanted to tell him what he needed to know. He wanted to know it. The problem was he was moving too fast and too much to listen. I finally grabbed him and held him still long enough to tell him the bathroom was on the outside. In a haste, he jerked free, bolted out the door, ran to the left, and disappeared around the building. I knew that he would be back.

I am not psychic or anything like that. I knew because the bathroom was on the other side of the building. My son was still only long enough to get part of the instruction.

Not much harm to him, just a lot of dancing around and some unnecessary running, but for me as his father, I was frustrated. I wanted to tell him where the bathroom was, if he had been still long enough I would have told him what he needed to know. If necessary, I would have shown him myself.

God is no different. Our heavenly Father wants to tell us things we need to know, but we are too busy doing important things to listen. Hurry, hurry, hurry, that's the way we live! Microwave, drive-thru(s), instant everything! Rush, rush, rush! Our lives are still not **better**, just **busier**. How frustrating it must be for God to want to tell us so much, show us so much, but we are too busy. My son finally found the bathroom on his own, but it came with lots of wasted effort, pain, and frustration.

Are you rushing past Godly instructions? Does your life consist of "things" that have to be done right now? Are you too busy to spend a half-hour in the morning or in the evening to be still and listen to God? My son stopped but only long enough to get part of the instructions. Being still long enough to receive some instruction is better than not being still at all, but not much better! You see giving someone direction requires time. God needs time with you to order your steps, light up your path, and guide your life.

We need to slow down! If you have been given the wrong directions running faster will only get you lost quicker. STOP! BE STILL! Before you move in any direction you must consult with your Heavenly Father. Slow down and your Father will instruct you. He will order your steps.

Good Steps are Ordered by the Lord

Let your heavenly Father instruct you *"the steps of a good man are ordered by the Lord" (Ps. 37:23).* When you allow the Lord to order your steps, he makes you into a good man. Having your steps ordered by Lord means more than simply having them directed. First, order means to have each step in the <u>proper place</u> in relationship with each other step. No one step you make is an independent step. Each step is predicated on the previous one as well as the one to follow. A good step leads to a good step. Good steps lead to a good man. Steps in the wrong direction will lead to other steps in the wrong direction. Daily time with your Heavenly Father allows him to correct wrong steps on a daily basis, and it gives you directions on the right steps to make. God orders your life one step at a time.

Secondly, when you say God orders your steps, what you are saying is God <u>organizes</u> them. Organization implies arranging them so that the whole works as a unit with each step having a proper function. Each individual step supports the journey as a whole. Direction must be clear. You must wait on direction from your Father before you move. Once a step is made, you must check back with the Father to ensure that step supports your journey as a whole. God alone knows the destination he has for you. You must seek him daily for instruction on the next step to make. He has the power and knowledge necessary to organize your steps and your life.

Finally, to have ordered steps mean to have them <u>arranged</u> by God. This requires relationship, sequence, and adjustments. Steps in the right direction are related; steps in the wrong direction are not. Steps ordered by God are related to other steps ordered by God. The steps you make in God have no relationship to the ones you make on your own. Having the right relationship between God and each step provides the right sequence for your steps. Some steps require you to pause before you take the next step. This waiting period is a part of God's plan. This ensures you arrive at the right destination at the right time. The pauses in your steps and in your life are ordered by the Lord and are a part of his plan. When the Lord arranges your steps, no adjustments are required. God does the arranging, sequencing, and adjusting. This builds the right relationship between you, your steps, and God. Remember *"For as many as are led by the spirit of God, they are the sons of God"* *(Romans 8:14).*

Slow down so your Father can order your steps. He should be the only one you allow to lead you into the plan he has for you. The Lord must order your steps. Slow down and receive your Father's instruction.

Father's Instruction

Solomon wrote *"Hear ye children the <u>instruction of a father</u>, and attend to know understanding. (Pr. 4:1).* Proverbs instruct children to hear their father's instructions. Hearing is non-optional. When you put yourself in your Father's presence, you are acknowledging you are there to hear. He is there to instruct you, not for you to instruct Him. Your Father already knows your needs. Now it's time for you to learn His will for you. By hearing his instruction, your problem and petitions will be fewer. You will have no need to ask him for anything. His instruction to you will direct you where you need to go to get what you need.

"Hear ye children the instruction of a father, and <u>attend to know understanding</u>. (Pr. 4:1). The second part of that verse refers to attending to know understanding. Attend means to pay attention to. You must focus on God to obtain understanding. Children attend (focus) on him as the source of understanding. No other source supercedes

the Father's understanding. He knows you the best and therefore he is the only reliable source of understanding. If you attend to understanding from any other person, place or thing, you are missing out on true understanding, which only comes from God. God is waiting to explain all he has for you. Spend time with him and he will show you things you have been waiting your whole life to know.

Want instruction? Be still! Want information? Be Quiet! Want to know where the bathroom is? Be quiet and listen to your father!

CHAPTER THREE

HOW DO I KNOW IT'S GOD TALKING

WISDOM IS THE PRINCIPLE THING, THEREFORE GET WISDOM, IN ALL THY GETTING GET UNDERSTANDING. (PROVERB 4:7)

A Still Small Voice

I remember as a little boy growing up and how it would rain outside. If it was just raining there was no problem, but if it was thundering and lighting we had to go inside our home. With seven of us inside the house with not much to do, it would get kind of loud and noisy. I can still hear my mother's voice shouting, "Shut-up—God is talking!." I always thought she meant the thunder and the lighting was God talking to us. I really thought God was mad at us. I thought he was yelling so loud that it sounded like thunder. Boy was I wrong. 1 King 19: 11,12 tells us God was not in the strong wind, the earthquake, or the fire, but in a still small voice. *And he said, go forth, and stand upon the mount before the LORD. And, behold, the*

LORD passed by, and a great and strong wind rent the mountains, and brake in pieces the rocks before the LORD; but the LORD was not in the wind: and after the wind an earthquake; but the LORD was not in the earthquake: And after the earthquake a fire; but the LORD was not in the fire: and after the fire a still small voice.

The thunder and lighting is not God talking to you. It is there to let you know he is getting ready to speak. God puts his word (Spirit) in your belly. *He that believeth on me, as the scripture hath said, out of his belly shall flow rivers of living water. (But this spake he of the Spirit, which they that believe on him should receive: for the Holy Ghost was not yet given; because that Jesus was not yet glorified (John 7:38,39).*

God speaks in a still small voice, not in thunder and lighting. If it is thundering and lighting in your life, be quiet, God is getting ready to speak to you! The thunder is the prelude to God speaking to you. The storm in your life is not the voice of the Lord. All the storming in your life is God's way of saying, be quiet, I want to tell you something. He is not angry with you. He is trying to get your attention, because he has something wonderful to tell you. He has wonderful things to show you. When God speaks, he uses that still small voice inside of you.

And with all thy getting get understanding (Proverb 4:7b). Proverbs instructs you to get understanding. When you have the wrong understanding, you look for God in the wrong places. Lack of understanding will cause you to look for God in things. It will have you looking for God in signs and wonders. You will find yourself looking for him in physic revelations. God does not use those things to speak to you. He speaks to you in a still small voice inside of you. Listen to that voice, God wants to talk to you.

How do I Know it's God Talking?

How do I know it is God talking? How does God speak in that still small voice? You will be able to distinguish between your own inner voice and God because God's voice lines up with the Bible. You must validate the voice inside of you with the Word of God. The two must agree. Your understanding should help you see God. It should help you hear him clearly. If the words you hear inside you are confusing you, they are not of God. The bible says, *"For God is not the author of confusion, but of peace, as in all churches of the saints." (1Cor 14:33).*

As I grew as a Christian, I found out through the scripture that God speaks into the spirit of a person. Out of your belly shall flow rivers of living water (John 7:38). Your belly is the center of your being, and it is where the word of God abides in you. The river of living water is the Holy Spirit. God gives you the Holy Spirit to live inside of you, and then God speaks to you by his Holy Spirit inside of you. God's word starts in your belly (spirit). His word is powerful, sharper that any two-edged sword (Hebrews 4:12). God speaks to you by placing his word in your belly. Your spirit is the place where God goes to commune with you. This is the heart of man. The word in your heart belongs to God. He hid it there so you would not sin against him. *Thy word have I hid in mine heart, that I might not sin against thee (Psalms 119:11).* You know the words you hear inside of you are God's word because they keep you from sinning against him.

God speaks to you by putting his word into your belly. John *7:38,39, He that believeth on me, as the scripture hath said, out of his belly shall flow rivers of living water. (But this spake he of the Spirit, which they that believe on him should receive: for the Holy Ghost was not yet given; because that Jesus was not yet glorified.* He is talking to you right now. His word inside of you is giving you peace. You know he is talking to you because you have peace inside of you. Peace like a river of living water flowing through you and refreshing you. When God talks, it refreshes you. When the devil talks it worries, tires, and confuses you. If you are confused, it is not God. If the things that are on your mind are wearing you out, they are of not God. God comes to build you up! He speaks from the inside out, not from the outside in. He reveals his word to your spirit. It may go against your flesh, but your flesh is contrary to God anyway. It desires the things of the world. If it is fleshly (worldly), then it is not of God. If it is contrary to the things of God or the word of God, it is not of God! God's words edify and build you up. You will know it is the word of God, because it builds you up in your spirit and gives you peace.

Prophesy

God also speaks to you through prophesy. Don't confuse prophesy with tongues. Prophesy and tongues are not the same, and do not have the same purpose. Prophesy is God talking to you through a person. Prophesy is given by God to edify the church. *He that speaketh in an unknown tongue edifieth himself; but he that <u>prophesieth edifieth the church</u> (1Cor 14:4).* Prophecy is greater than tongues. It is equal to tongues plus interpretation. *I would that ye all spake with tongues, but rather that ye prophesied: <u>for greater is he that prophesieth than he that speaketh with tongues</u>, except he interpret, that the church may receive edifying (1 Cor 14:5).* Prophesy edifies, comforts, and exhorts the hearers and not the speaker. *But he that prophesieth speaketh unto men to edification, and exhortation, and comfort (1 Cor 14:3).* You know it is God speaking because the words are interpreted, and they comfort, edify, and exhort the church.

Tongues

Tongues are not God's word. They are the response to the word God has placed in your belly. They have their place in the body of Christ and should be encouraged, but not over prophesy. *I would that ye all spake with tongues, but rather that ye prophesied: for greater is he that prophesieth than he that speaketh with tongues, except he interpret, that the church may receive edifying (1Cor 14:5).* When a person speaks in tongues, they are talking to God and not to men. *For he that speaketh in an unknown tongue speaketh not unto men, but unto God: for no man understandeth him; howbeit in the spirit he speaketh mysteries (1Cor 14:2).* Tongues are you talking to God, not God talking to you. It is your response to the river of living water flowing through you. Tongues require no interpretation. They are given to edify the speaker and not the hearers. *He that speaketh in an unknown tongue edifieth himself (1Cor 14:4).* Tongues are the results of God's word springing up in your belly.

God puts his word in your belly (spirit) to build you up. Tongues come as a result of that word over flowing in you. Jude 1:20 says you build up your most holy faith praying in the Holy Ghost. When you pray in tongues your faith is built up. Tongues have their place in the body of Christ, and as long as they are done decently and in order, they should never be forbidden. *Wherefore, brethren, covet to prophesy, and forbid not to speak with tongues. Let all things be done decently and in order (1Cor 14:39,40).*

How do you know its God talking? You know it is God talking because the Bible validates the word inside you. It works from the inside out, building you up. God's words edify, exhort and comfort. His words cause you not to sin against him. His word teaches you how to be quiet, so you can hear what his Holy Spirit is saying to your spirit.

This is how you know God is talking to you. When God is talking, your spirit, soul and body is quiet before him. Once you learn to recognize God's voice, you have a powerful weapon to use against the enemy.

God's Words are Mighty

Being quiet before the Lord is a weapon. It is not a carnal weapon, but it is a weapon. *For the weapons of our warfare are not carnal, but mighty through God to the pulling down of strong holds (2Cor 10:4).* God's Word leads you around the enemies' traps. When Moses went before the Lord he received the instruction necessary to lead the children of Israel out of Egypt. The Lord warned Elisha about the traps being set against the children of Israel. *Then the king of Syria warred against Israel, and took counsel with his servants, saying, In such and such a place shall be my camp. And the man of God sent unto the king of Israel, saying, Beware that thou pass not such a place; for thither the Syrians are come down. And the king of Israel sent to the place which the man of God told him and warned him of, and saved himself there, not once nor twice.* Being quiet is a weapon. It is how we get instructions. God's instructions (words) are powerful, sharper than a two-edged sword (Hebrew 4:12). What a mighty weapon we have. It may not be a weapon you can see, but it is mighty through God.

Satan does not want you to be quiet. He does not want God to give you his word to use as a weapon against him. He is always seeking to attack you. satan attacks you through your mind. He bombards you with thoughts, images, and sounds that are contrary to the word God has hidden in your heart (spirit). He uses people, television, radio, magazines, books, and any other object available to attack your mind. Even your sleep time is not immune to his attack. How do you combat him? How do you counter his attack? "Conscious Rest" is one way of countering his attack. When you meditate on the Lord you take active control of your mind. You are in the driver's seat. You are able to steer your mind in a direction that leads to God. When you do this, peace will overtake you. God will take over your mind and you will be able to rest. *Thou wilt keep him in perfect peace, whose mind is stayed on thee: because he trusteth in thee (Isaiah 26:3).*

God's Word Gives Peace

"Conscious rest," is the ability to rest in the Lord's arms while you are in a conscious state. God wants to give you peace while you are awake. Conscious rest, means to have your mind stayed on the Lord. If your mind is stayed on him, then your peace will be perfect. You are quieting your mind when it is stayed on the Lord. There is a benefit to having a quiet mind. You quiet the mind and God will quiet the man. You give the Lord a quiet mind and he will give you a quiet man. God will also give that man a quiet spirit. A quiet man has a quiet spirit. He has peace within himself. He does not worry about what will be. He knows that God will give him his daily bread this day. The ability to rest in the Lord has been given to you. You can abide under the shadow of his wing.

Study to be quiet means to study "perfect peace." Perfect peace is uninterrupted peace. It is continual peace. Peace like a river. This means your peace will flow into more peace. Your peace will be perfect. Perfect peace is correct peace. Peace that gives God glory. If you are seeking peace in any other source other than God, you are not seeking perfect peace. The church is your sanctuary, but God is your peace.

Go to church and spend time with the Father. Spend time alone with the Lord. You cannot get perfect peace by going to church alone. You have to spend time with the Father to get your peace perfected. Church is for worship. It is a time of giving back to God. Time spent at church will edify you. Time spent with the Father will perfect you. Time spent at church will refresh you. Time spent with the Father will revive you. Both are necessary. Church keeps your spirit alive. God keeps your peace alive within your soul. His peace is the right peace. His peace is everlasting. His peace is perfect. You combat the devil that wars against your mind with the perfect peace you get by keeping your mind stayed on God.

CHAPTER FOUR

MAKING YOUR WAY PROSPEROUS

This book of the law shall not depart out of thy mouth, but you shall <u>meditate</u> in it day and night, that you may observe to do according to all that is written in it. For then you will make your way prosperous, and then you will have good success (Joshua 1:8). The book of the law is the word of God. There is a reason we are meditating on the word of God. Joshua states meditating on the word and observing to do the word will make your way prosperous and you will have good success. When you study the word and the will of the Father you become successful. As a matter of fact you become <u>very</u> successful. Good success is a by-product of meditating on the word.

God wants you to be prosperous. There is no doubt about that. He not only wants you to be prosperous, but he also provides you with the provision to become clean. <u>Study to Be Quiet is that provision!</u> Remember, study to be quiet is still quiet reflection or contemplation on God, or to put it simply, quietly listening to God. Listening to

God! God does the leading, and you do the following. This will cleanse your ways. You are probably saying "God was leading me the entire time." I don't need to be quiet for God to lead me. Wrong! Remember we change everyday. New thoughts, new actions, new habits are created. These daily changes require daily evaluations.

New Mind

As a newborn Christian your spirit is born again, but your body and souls are not. You still have the same mind and the same body. Jesus spoke in *John 3:5 "unless a man be born of the water and the spirit he cannot enter the kingdom of God."* The water represents the Holy Spirit! In *John 7:38* Jesus spoke of the Holy Spirit rolling out of a man's belly like rivers of living <u>water</u>. Paul wrote, it is the same Spirit which raised Christ from the dead which shall quicken (make alive) your mortal bodies. Your <u>spirit</u> is being made alive (born again) by the Holy Spirit. Hallelujah! I like the sound of that! God's Holy Spirit making my spirit alive again.

What about my mind, how does it get renewed? The answer is found in the word of God.

"<u>Let</u> us be not conformed to this world, but let us be transformed by the renewing of your mind" (Romans 12:2).

Knowledge changes a person's way of thinking. When you know better, it enables you to do better. Your mind needs to be fed righteous thoughts. Righteous thoughts come from God. His thoughts are not your thoughts. Your thoughts need to be transformed. God transformed Saul's thoughts on the road to Damascus. Saul's thoughts were to persecute the church. God's thoughts were to protect it. After just one conversation with Jesus, Saul's mind was changed. He was transformed. This transformation was a result of knowledge. He met

Jesus and from that moment forward Saul saw Jesus differently. Knowledge changes a person's way of thinking. When you spend time with the Father, you will know his thoughts, and your mind will be renewed. Getting your mind renewed is the beginning of making your way prosperous.

"Let this mind be in you that was also in Christ Jesus" (Phil. 2:5)

Prosperity begins from within you. Your new mind begins with you. You have to do the letting! Your old way of thinking has to be replaced with a new way of thinking. Your spirit is clean, but your mind still needs to be renewed. Your spirit is clean, but your mind needs to be transformed. Your spirit is clean, but your mortal body needs to be raised. Let God cleanse your spirit, soul and body. When God's word becomes a part of you, you have the mind of Christ. Let Jesus' mind be in you.

God Wants to Preserve You

Now may the God of peace Himself sanctify you completely; and may your whole spirit, soul, and body be preserved blameless at the coming of the Lord Jesus Christ. (1Thes. 5:23)

God wants to preserve you. What do you want? Your desire is a part of the process. The children of Israel desired a king, but God desired to be their king. They got what they desired. God does not force his desires on you. You will get what you desire. God is going to do it. You just have to desire it also. You have to do more than just say it. You have to put yourself in the position, posture, and the place for God to do the work. God needs individual time with you to preserve you individually. God wants quiet time with you so he can preserve you completely.

and may your whole spirit, soul, and body be preserved blameless at the coming of the Lord Jesus Christ. (1Thes. 5:23)
Your spirit, soul and body need to be preserved. That is a lot of work! That requires more time than what you put in at church. To clean a person's spirit you need to get the cleaner (word) to the heart (spirit) of the matter. The word needs time to soak in. Outside of God, your spirit has not been preserved. It has been exposed to all kind of things. Without God instructing you continually, your heart will get weathered, worn, and bitter. A bitter heart leads to a bitter person.

It is very important for you to keep your heart from being weathered. The heart is the key. Once the heart goes the body is soon to follow. The body stops functioning shortly after the heart stops beating. After a few hours the body becomes rigid and difficult to move. The body needs the heart and the heart needs God. God wants your heart to be clean so your body will not die. He wants you to live in him and enjoy the things he has for you. God has plans to prosper your heart.

Voice of God

You need to hear from God in order to prosper. Sometimes it seems difficult to hear from God. You often are confused by all the noise you hear inside and outside of yourself. There are so many distractions. Each day is full of things and events that sound like God. The devil is constantly sending out misinformation as well. Now the question is, how do I create an environment to hear from God? You can look to the children of Israel. They heard from God in their wilderness experience more than all other times in the Bible combined.

Your study of being quiet must include separation, silence, and stillness. You cannot here God in a crowd so you must **separate** yourselves from Egypt. **Silence** is also necessary because you can not hear clearly if you are talking. Finally, if you are not **still,** you will move past God's instruction. *The voice of God can be heard at the place where separation, silence, and stillness interact.* This is that quiet place in your heart where you hear God. When God spoke to Elijah, he was neither in the fire nor in the earthquake, but in a still small voice. Learning how to bring these three elements together is a process that every Christian must learn if they are to effectively hear from God.

God wants you to prosper. When you meditate on God's word and do what is written, you become very successful. The things you need to know in order to be successful are in God. He will make your way prosperous. Separation, silence, and stillness are part of hearing the voice of God. Over the next few chapters, we will study each one individually.

CHAPTER FIVE

SEPARATION: COME OUT FROM AMONG THEM

Separating yourself from the rest of the world is one of the most important things you can do as a believer. Our misdirection, failures, inconsistencies, and sins all can be traced back to not spending enough time alone with God. Spending time in church and spending time with God are two different things. Church is for worshipping God and receiving instruction corporately. Every father should spend time with his children as a family and as an individual. Our heavenly father is no different. Quality time with the Father at church and at home is essential.

You Need to be Alone with God

Moses with all of the best teaching that Egypt could offer still needed time alone with God. Moses was raised in pharaoh's house. He had the best upbringing his time could offer. For forty years he enjoyed a luxurious life among the Egyptians, but before God could use him he had to separate him. So after forty years in the oasis of Egypt, God sends him to the backside of the wilderness.

The wilderness is a place absent from distractions. This is the place God sends His people to alone with Him. Cleansing requires separation!

Moses' wilderness experience was a part of God's plan. Fresh out of Egypt, he had a lot of Egypt still in him. He still had on Egypt's clothing. Not to mention he was also mistaken for an Egyptian by one of the women of Midian. Prior to leaving Egypt, Moses murdered an Egyptian and was on the run from the law. To make matters worse, his secret was exposed about he not being the son of Pharaoh. So God sent him to the wilderness to clean him up. In the wilderness none of those things mattered. When God takes a person to the wilderness; he is taking him there to strip him of all the things that do not matter. All the experiences we have outside of God do not matter. Your wilderness cleanses you of "stuff" that will hinder the new you. Moses was not in the wilderness; he was in the plan of God.

Like Moses, your wilderness experience is a part of God's plan. We all have a past that comes up from time to time to haunt us. We all have things in our past that will not help us fulfill the plan of God. Maybe like Moses, you have had a run in with the law. God wants to take you to the wilderness to take care of that. Your title, position, or status does not matter to God. He knows the real you. He must send you to the wilderness so he can show you who you are in Him. When you learn who you are in him you will no longer need all that other "stuff." That other "stuff" is just an opportunity for people to get a stronghold on you.

You are naked before an all knowing God. You will finally see your true self. Sometimes this can be depressing. Your self-esteem may become low because a man is always humbled before an all-knowing God. That is why some people don't like being alone with God. It is hard to see the true side of yourself and not be humbled. Like Moses, you will have to lose your status to see God. By being free of all that "stuff," you will be able to find the real you like Moses did. Then you will be able to go back to Egypt and get what belongs to you. You will be able to get your family back. Moses went back to Egypt and led the children of Israel to the promise land. No matter how difficult, your wilderness is a part of God's plan.

Separation and Cleansing Go Hand In Hand

Sanctify them through thy truth, thy word is truth John 17:17

I was in an automobile with a man who obviously had been drinking. The smell of alcohol was coming out of every orifice of his body. He was even sweating alcohol through his pores. His body was using all it's resources to expel the alcohol out. Expulsion of waste is a natural function of the body. If he stopped drinking alcohol, his body would eventually expel it all out. Separating himself from alcohol must take place before his body, or even God could cleanse him. Stop eating and drinking the wrong foods and your body will automatically expel the bad food out of itself. You cannot be cleansed from bad things if you are constantly putting bad things into your body. Separate yourself from food. Your body needs to cleanse itself.

Fasting from food is a part of God's plan. God instructs us to fast. When you fast from food you bring your body into subjection. The strongest desire in the body is the desire for food. You can go longer without sex, money, power, complements, employment, and fame, than you can without food. When you control your desire for food, you make all your other desires get in line. The desire for food is the strong man that must be bound. All other desires will get in line. Go on a fast and you will not have the time or the desire to seek other things. All your thoughts will be on food. Your conversation will be about places to eat. When you are on a fast, your friends will start looking like food. All you will be able to think about is food. All your other desires will be in line behind the desire to eat. That is why fasting is a part of God's plan for you. That which works for the body also works for the mind. Watching or reading the wrong things will only corrupt the mind. As the saying goes, garbage in, garbage out. Quiet time with God cleanses the mind. It clears the soul of impure thoughts and the spirit of impure actions. God wants to expel all of the bad "stuff" out of the inner man, the real you. Stop feeding your body hate, racism, jealousy, envy, and anger and your body will expel out those things as well. Consider the following scriptures:

Come out from among them and be ye <u>separate</u>, says the Lord. And touch not the unclean thing. And I <u>will</u> be a Father to you and you <u>will</u> be my sons and daughters" (2 Cor 6:17).

Not touching things is a form of separation. We are to only touch, handle, or entertain clean things. We are instructed to "Come out from among them." The "them" in this scripture is referring to unclean things. Remember that they are too numerous to list, so let God be your father and He will take care of the rest. Once you have touched God nothing unclean will ever do. Being in the presence of the Lord is what your spirit, soul, and body desires. I had the opportunity to be caught up in the spirit in the presence of the Lord. I wanted to stay there in his presence. My thoughts were clean, my mind was clean, and my heart was clean. Being with God is how we touch him. Touch God. He is clean; He is Holy. Come out from among them because separation and cleansing go hand and hand.

Whatsoever things are true, whatsoever things are honest, whatsoever things are just, whatsoever things are pure, whatsoever things are lovely, whatsoever things are of a good report, if there be any virtue, and if there be any praise, think on these things. (Phil 4:8)

This scripture calls on you to separate yourself from bad thoughts by thinking good thoughts. It does not list the bad things we should not be thinking on. That would take too long and the list would be constantly changing. This verse gives you eight things you should be thinking on. Separation should never be look on from a negative perspective. You should not be worrying about what you will be giving up, or what you should not be thinking on. If you simply do what the word says and "Think on these things," you will not have time to think on anything else.

The children of Israel did not lose the pleasure of Egypt, they gained the fellowship of God. I want you to spend time with your Heavenly Father as a form of rewarding yourself. You are in the world everyday, getting worldly thoughts and worldly ways. I am not asking you to give up on the world. I am asking you to spend time with the Father and he will give you the world. He will give you the desires of your heart. But if you seek to save your life, you will lose it, and if you lose your life for Christ sake, you will save it.

Come out from among them and God <u>will</u> be your father and you <u>will</u> be his sons and daughters. God cleansed Elijah from his fear by sending him on a forty days journey to the Mount of God. Once he arrived there God told him to turn around and go back. Why did God have him travel all that way only to tell him to turn around and go back? God wanted quiet time alone with him. During those forty days of being separated, God was able to cleanse him of his fear and prepare him for his next task. Are you fearful about your future? Spend some time alone with God. He will be your Father. He will nurture you, guide you, and help you. You will be his child, able to call upon Him in your time of need.

God's Peace Guards Your Heart

...And the peace of God, which surpasses all under-standing, will guard your hearts and minds through Christ Jesus. (Phil. 4:7)

Separation brings peace. God wants to guard your heart and mind through Jesus Christ. God wants to protect your spirit, intellect, emotions, and your will. This can only be accomplished through Jesus. He is the Good Shepherd. All others are thieves, robbers, and hirelings. They have not given their lives for you. Peace comes from God. He gives it to you to keep you.

Jesus "The Word" guards you from all the things that will oppose your peace. He shall keep you in perfect peace, whose mind is stayed on him. God's peace is perfect, and it surpasses all understanding. It can not be comprehended. Time with your Heavenly Father is peaceful time. He stands guard so you can rest. Jesus stands as a strong tower between you and the things that oppose your peace. He has a quiet peaceful place for you under the shadow of his wing. Peace is the result of separating yourself from the world to be alone with God.

God's peace kept Noah. Noah was in a wicked environment. He was under physical and spiritual attack. God needed to separate him so he could guard his mind and clean up his environment. Noah was separated from the rest of the world by forty days of rain. He, his family and a bunch of animals were all alone. Isolated from the world and its' substances, they were forced to depend on God!

While Noah and his family lived in a tiny ark, separated from all others, God was cleaning his environment! Want God to cleanse your environment? Separate yourself! By separating yourself, you will be guarding your heart and mind. God's peace kept Noah, and it will do the same for you.

Wilderness and Your Relationships

So he himself often withdrew into the wilderness and prayed. (Luke 5:16)

Jesus used the wilderness to separate himself from the world to have quiet time with the Father. He sent the children of Israel there, and now he wants to send you there. The wilderness is your uncultivated and uninhabited experience. It involves your **relationships**. In those periods of extreme loneliness, God wants to use that time to talk to you. That broken relationship is the perfect opportunity to be alone with the Father. Jesus often withdrew into the wilderness. No friends, no family, just him and the Father. If you are currently not in a relationship, you are in the wilderness, and God wants to talk to you. Being alone with yourself is OK. Your wilderness experience is necessary for your Father to talk to you. Don't fight it just enjoy it. You have time alone with the Father and no other relationship can compare to that.

All of your relationships will be better after you have been with the Father. You will be easier to get along with. All the stuff that opposes your peace will be removed. You will be able to see yourself clearly and therefore see others clearly as well. Spend time with the Father and he will instruct you on how to correct problems with your marriage. He will show you how to deal with your children, job and church members. Being by yourself with the Lord will help you be with others. Your wilderness is waiting for you so God can bless your other relationships.

Desert and Your Substance

Now when it was day, he departed and went into a deserted place. (Luke 4:42)
God also uses the <u>desert</u> for you to be alone with him. It involves your **substances or physical material**. The desert is an unproductive environment. God takes you there sometimes just to talk to you. You experience setback and loss in your life. You know that all thing work for the good to them that love the Lord. This should be a time for you to go to the Father and get instructions from him. The desert experience is not there to punish you. Your substance can keep you from seeing the Father. Knowing God better is more important than having stuff. Spending time with the Father during loss, setbacks, death, failed business, or bad experiences, will give the devil a black eye and maximize your desert experience. God took the children of Israel into the desert to bless them. He blessed their <u>substance</u>. Spend time with the Father and turn material loss into spiritual gain.

Jesus was baptized in the river Jordan and the Holy Spirit descended on him like a dove. He was anointed by God to go out and begin his ministry. The first thing the Holy Spirit did was to lead him into the desert to be alone with God. The Holy Ghost did not lead him to church to preach his initial sermon. He did not lead him into the streets to heal the sick. Jesus was anointed to go, but he knew he needed time alone with the Father. The desert is the beginning of ministry. You cannot minister without going through the desert. Your substances need to be sanctified. The children of Israel received the Commandments in the desert. God is waiting to give you his commandment for you. He is waiting to instruct you on what he wants you to do.

Mountain and Your Self-esteem

He went up on a mountain __by himself__ to pray. And when evening had come, he was alone there (Mt.14: 23).

The mountain involves your **self-esteem**. When you are on the mountaintop everything goes your way. From this high position you can see the land of promise. You know your blessings are on the way, and you see the land flowing with milk and honey. You can also see the traps of the enemy. When you are on the mountaintop, everyone knows you. You are on display. Your self-esteem is at its highest. You are happy. God wants to talk to you when you are happy. There are things he wants to show you that you will have to be on the mountaintop to see. You need time alone with the Father on your mountain. Jesus knew this. He could have taken his disciples with him. This could have been an excellent opportunity for him to teach them about prayer. But Jesus knew teaching them would have taken time away from being alone with the Father. Time alone with the Father was more important to Jesus than teaching his disciples. There would be time for him to teach later, but for now, just enjoy the Father.

Alone with Self

But when thou prayest, __enter into thy closet__, and when thou has shut thy door, pray to thy Father which is __in secret__; and thy Father which seeth in secret shall __reward thee openly__ (Matt 6:6)

Jesus spent time alone with the Father in the morning and the evening. He spent time alone with him in the wilderness, desert, and the mountain. Now Jesus is asking you to go to your closet (devotional chamber), and pray in secret (alone), and your Father will reward you openly. There is a reward to you for spending time alone with the Father. Everyone will be able to see your reward. All will know that you are blessed. It will show in your relationship, substance, and self-esteem. It will show in your countenance. Everyone will be able to tell you have been alone with the Father. *"... And they took knowledge of them, that they had been with Jesus,"* Acts 4:13.

Think about what God did for the children of Israel. They were in a desert, solitary place, isolated from the rest of the world. No shopping, sewing, cooking, just waiting on the Father to clothe and feed them. Their only distraction was the golden calf they created with their own hands. They had become accustomed to life in Egypt (bondage) so much that when God removed them from Egypt to the wilderness, they made the wilderness Egypt. When God blesses you with quiet time to be alone with him don't turn on the TV or the radio and bring Egypt into your solitude. Sit still, be quiet and enjoy being alone with the Father. Learn to love your own company. If you don't enjoy being alone with yourself, will anyone else enjoy being alone with you? Solitude is an essential part of self to self-alignment and daily cleansing. Remember, no television, friends, or family, just you and the Lord. If you can learn to love being alone with yourself chances are everyone else will also. Separation (being alone with God) and cleansing go hand and hand. Time alone with God will help you love yourself.

Now when it was day, he departed and went into a deserted place. (Luke 4:42)

Jesus enjoyed being by himself. He knew the Father would meet him there. He needed to get away from the crowd. No church service, club, team, or organization could take the place of time alone the Father. Jesus valued his time with God. He got up early in the morning to be alone with him. He went to the desert, mountain, and the wilderness. He was setting an example for us. God wants to be alone with you. You cannot be alone with God at church. You need a prayer closet. You need a devotional chamber. God wants to have time with you all to himself. Find a place to be alone with the Father. Separation does not mean you are alone. Your Father will join you if you invite him.

CHAPTER SIX

SILENCE: STUDY TO BE QUIET

STUDY TO BE QUIET (1 THES 4:11)

Silence is Golden

Someone once wrote silence is golden. In other words silence is a precious commodity. *"The words of the wise men are heard in <u>quiet</u> more than the cry of him that ruleth among fools" Ecc. 9:17.* 1Peter 4:4 says a meek and quiet spirit was of great price in the sight of God. It is something that should be sought after. There was <u>silence</u> in heaven about the space of a half-hour (Rev 8:1). *Be <u>silent</u>, all flesh before the Lord. Zec 2:13.* All flesh is to be silent before God. The Bible says for you to "study to be quiet." Being quiet does not come on its' own, you have to study it. The word study means to consider attentively or in detail. With that in mind, let's consider attentively what the Bible says about being quiet.

Study to be quiet means to study to be at peace. This is more than not talking. Your mouth could be silent, but your soul could be in torment. Your mouth could be silent, but your body could be raging. You need to learn how to quiet your body, soul, and spirit. Study to be quiet means you are at peace with God. Peace with God brings about peace with self. Peace with self brings about a quiet spirit. A quiet spirit leads to a quiet person. When a man's ways please God even his enemy will be at peace with him, and more importantly, he will be at peace with himself.

He who Guards His Mouth Preserves His Life

Thou are snared with the words of thy mouth; thou are taken with the words of thy mouth. (Proverb 6:2) The words you speak can snare you. It can get you tangled up. The more you talk, the greater the chance of you getting snared and taken. The word taken implies being captured. You can be captured by your own words. When you speak, you put spiritual principles into action. You cause a spiritual chain reaction. You can blow yourself up by speaking the wrong things that are not of God. When you keep your mouth you guard your life. Silence is a one way of not blowing yourself up. You cannot be snared by words not spoken. Keeping silent preserves your life.

For over 400 years the children of Israel cried out to God out of Egypt. The crying did not cease day or night for God to deliver them from their evil taskmasters. God told Moses he had heard their crying. Was God being silent for 400 years? Of course not! He is nigh unto them of a humble and contrite spirit. God sent Moses to give them what the asked for. He sent Moses to deliver them from their evil taskmasters.

False Promises Hinder God

If you make promises to God that you do not keep that hinders him from moving on your behalf. When you tell God you will do something if he gets you out of your situation; he expects you to do it. He waits patiently for you to do what you said you would do it. He cannot move until you complete your promise. This slows down the plan of God. It is better not to promise than to promise and not keep it. When you talk too much, you slow down the plan of God. Moses' silence won favor with God. He heard God for the entire nation of Israel. They were to busy crying out and making promises. Moses did not promise God anything. He was silent, and he was able to hear the plan God had for him and the Children of Israel.

When you do not keep your promises, it creates a moral dilemma for God. When you don't do what you say, you lie to God. Lying is a sin and sin separates you from God. He would have blessed you had you not promised, but now he has to deal with the sin. It is like a child coming to his father for something. If he lies to get what he wants, he will not get what he was seeking and will be disciplined as well. His father had no intention of disciplining him. The child was punished because of his own words. Your words will snare you. They will get you disciplined at times when your father had no intentions of punishing you. You don't have to make promises. You only have to ask. Your Father is waiting to bless you. He is waiting to give you what you need.

God Heard Your Call

God said in *Isaiah 65:24 before they call, I will answer; and while you are yet speaking I will hear you.* God heard you while you were speaking. He answered you before you called. God already has an answer for you. He answered you when you called. You probably did not hear him. You were probably telling him about your troubles. He heard you a long time ago. He is waiting to give you the answer. Study to be quiet. Learn how to get the answers you need from God. Get the answer from Him for today's problem before you tell him about tomorrow's. Remember that he has already heard you and he is patiently waiting to answer you.

He said again in Isaiah; *"Behold, the Lord's hand is not shortened, that it can not save; neither is his ear heavy, that he cannot hear: (Isaiah 59:1).* God can hear! We need to be quiet so we can hear his answer. *Isaiah 7:4* tells us to *" take heed and be quiet."* This means to pay attention and be quiet. Being quiet is one part of hearing, and paying attention is the other part. God wants your focus to be on Him. Be quiet and give God your attention. When you study to be quiet, you study how to pay attention to God.

Moses was able to hear God, but not in Egypt. There was too much noise and activity there. God had to take him to the backside of the desert to speak to him. No noise there, no activities, just the voice of God. Moses left his father-in-laws house, the servants, and the sheep to be alone with God. Silently, he approached an amazing sight. A bush that was burning but not consumed. Out of this bush God spoke to him. Had he been talking or even praying he would have missed his opportunity to hear from God. The book of Revelation speaks of those who have an "ear to hear" or a listening ear. They are the ones who will hear what the spirit has to say to the church. Silence is our way of saying, *"Speak Lord for thy servant hearth"* (1Sam 3:9). We cannot talk and listen at the same time. Be quiet, God is talking to you!

Silence in Heaven and in Earth

And there was silence in Heaven about the space of a half-hour. (Rev 8:1)
Silence is golden. There was silence in heaven. Even heaven must give way to silence. God was about to speak and all heaven must pay attention. You must be quiet when God is talking. There was silence in heaven for about a half-hour. Use this as a starting point. Spend a half-hour in the morning with your Heavenly Father. He will reward you openly for the time you spend with him secretly.

And he was there with the Lord forty days and forty nights; he did neither eat bread, nor drink water. And he wrote upon the tables the words of the covenant, the Ten Commandments. (Exodus 34:28). Exodus records for 40 days God spoke to Moses concerning the children of Israel. God gave him the laws and statutes to give to his children. He shared his plans for Israel. Oh, how excited he was to share the wonderful things he had planned for them. Moses went without breaks for meals, water, or trips to the bathroom. This time with the Father was too important for Moses to focus on fleshly needs. He was alone with the Father. He was there for forty days and he was not hungry.

He would have stayed longer. Exodus 32:7,8 shows us it was the noise of the children of Israel that interrupted this all-important meeting. Their lack of silence caused God's conversation with Moses to be cut short. Silence is golden. It not only allows you to hear from God, but it also allows others to hear as well. Keep silent during worship, Bible study, and Sunday school so others can hear what the Lord is saying. Study to be quiet! Consider attentively being quiet. God wants your undivided attention. Keeping your tongue is a part of worshipping God. You cannot be quiet without taming your tongue.

Tame Your Tongue

The tongue is an unruly member, who can tame it?
(James 3:8) Tame your tongue. It is not disciplined. It is
not submissive to authority. You have to tame it. You have
to humble it. You discipline your tongue by making it be
silent. You tame it by harnessing it. Being quiet tames the
tongue. You bring it into subjection. Your tongue will want
to rebel, but you can tame it. Time alone with the Father
tames your tongue.

It is a little member and boasteth great things (James
4:5). It defileth the whole body (James 4:6). The tongue is little, but it boasts great things. It will give glory to itself.
The more you talk the more glory you will give to yourself. The tongue exaggerates. It will make you into the mar-
tyr. It makes little things into big things. If you don't tame
your tongue it will eventually boast of itself to God. Tame
your tongue! This will preserve your body and your soul.
Remember silence is golden, so study to be quiet.

Jesus ruled his tongue. He spent 40 days in
the desert alone with God. The scriptures do not record
one word that was said by Jesus during that time. Not one
word in 40 days! Jesus was showing us through this pas-
sage of scripture that spending forty days listening to God
is better the spending 40 days talking to God. He talked
to the Father when he prayed for his disciples, but he lis-
tened to the Father all night before he chose them. (Luke
6:12,13) Jesus ruled his tongue. *Now in the morning hav-*
ing risen along while <u>before daylight</u>, He went out and
departed to a solitary place; and there he prayed (Mark 2:35).
Again, nothing is recorded in the scripture being said. Now,
I was not there and I don't know for sure if anything was
said or not, but I am sure nothing was recorded as being
said. Those scriptures paint a picture of Jesus spending time
<u>listening</u> to the Father! Jesus prayer involved him listening

to God, not talking. He was setting an example for us to follow.

Listening to God makes you golden. Your silence will keep you. God will preserve your heart and soul. His instruction will give you life. He is always looking ahead of you. He is mapping out your tomorrow. God will tell you where your blessings are located. He will tell you how to prosper. He will reward you openly for the time you spend with him in secret. God has so much to tell you. He is waiting for you to listen so he can share with you how he is going to make you as pure gold. Silence is golden.

CHAPTER SEVEN

STILLNESS: GOD IS NOT A BILLBOARD

BE STILL AND KNOW THAT I AM GOD (PSALMS 46:10)

When you are quiet and free of motion you can know God. You will be able to understand who he really is to you. Have you every passed a billboard on the highway? How much information were you able to grasp. You probably were able to notice the obvious things, but to really see the details you would have to slow down. If you were going to read the fine print on that billboard you need to come to a complete stop. How can you get all that God wants to show you moving all the time? You can only get a glimpse if you are not still. You cannot see the salvation of the Lord if you are not still. God wants you to be still so you can know him. He wants you to be still so you can understand him. He is not a billboard rush past. He is a work of art. He is the Lord Almighty. Stop and reverence him. God wants to show you his handiwork.

The Real You

God wants to show you yourself as he sees you. The world has shown you the wrong you. Be still and know God and he will show you the real you. The real you is blessed and is able to bless others. The real you will lead a nation out of Egypt. You don't need Pharaoh's clothing. God has riches for you that are beyond what the world has to offer. You are more than what you see in the mirror in the morning. Moses spent time with God, and God showed Moses himself. Be still and know God. The real you is waiting to meet you.

Every major prophet in the Bible practices the art of being still before God. Some of them would lay prostrate before God or sit in sackcloth and ashes. In this position of humility they would wait patiently on him. It was in their stillness that God was able to strengthen them.

They that wait upon the Lord shall mount up with wings of eagles, they shall run and not be weary, and they shall walk and not faint (Isaiah 40:31). They waited and were strengthen. Waiting is strength. Being still before the Lord strengthens you. Stillness is the way you mount up with wings of eagles. Being still is the way you run without being weary. Running without direction from the Lord will tire you out. Being still is the way you walk without fainting. Every step that is directed by the Lord is a good step. Good steps don't have to be repeated. They don't make you weary. Waiting is being still. Being still is waiting. Both give you strength. You will be able to soar above your situation. You will be able to know God.

Being Still but Active

The steps of a good man are ordered by the Lord. (Ps. 37:23) Stillness does not mean you are inactive. Inactivity is death. Dead things are still and inactive. You are to be still, but you are not to be inactive. You are moving. Your steps are under God's control. Your impulse and inclination are under his control. He controls your motion. Stillness declares God to be the one who orders your steps. Your activity is in God. Your thoughts lead to the Lord. Your "will" leads to the Lord. You are still, but your mind is stayed on him. You are still, but you are thinking on good things. You are still, but your steps are ordered by the Lord. No good thing will he withhold from them that walk upright.

Movement without direction leads to wasted energy and effort. You weaken your walk with God by moving forward without his leading. How many times have you ventured away from God's will, only to have to return to the same place you were before? Be still. Stillness is a part of cleansing as well. You can never recharge without being still. You can never enjoy the beauty of a star filled night with out being still! You can never enjoy the wonderful symphony of nature without being still. Each movement requires energy, and each utterance requires effort. I must be still! I know that God is not a billboard. I am still, but I am active.

Continued movement requires continued energy. I must be silent! Continued utterance requires continued effort! Potential energy requires the object to be at rest. To tap into your true potential you must learn the art of *"conscious rest."* Sleep requires energy. If you sleep too much you will wake up tired. Quiet time with God gives you energy. Your full potential becomes possible! Your mind becomes sharper, your thoughts become clear, and your actions become purposed! Being still before the Lord is the way you recharge your mind. This is mandatory. If your mind is allowed to run continuously, it will burn out. When your mind burns out, your body gives out. You must be still. Your mind and body need to rest in the Lord.

Stillness Allows God to Lead You

Which the LORD commanded Moses in mount Sinai, in the day that he commanded the children of Israel to offer their oblations unto the LORD, in the wilderness of Sinai (Lev 7:38).

The children of Israel spent 400 years in Egypt working night and day. This resulted in 400 years of them being too busy and too tired to hear from God. They were working too hard, crying too loud, and moving too much to hear God's voice. God was not in the earthquake, nor in the wind, nor in the fire, but in a still small voice. They had become a people of perpetual motion. God was going to take them out of Egypt and still their movement. Every movement they took from henceforth would be with his leading. He would go before them in a pillar of cloud by day and a pillar of fire by night. They would remain in place until God moved them to the next place they should be. Because they follwed God's lead, their clothes never wore out! They did not have to work for food; God fed them himself. They heard from God more during this time than all the other times in the Bible combined. They were given the commandments. God met with them every day. He was a very present help in the time of need. He provided daily instructions on what they needed to do in order to live. Stillness provides God the opportunity to instruct you. *Be still and know I am God (Psalms 46:10).* Daily quiet time places you in the position, and the place to hear from God daily! God wants to slow you down so he can commune with you. He wants to give you the instruction you need to live the life he has planned for you.

Stillness Allows You to Hear the Lord

And Moses said unto them, <u>stand still</u>, and I will hear what the LORD will command concerning you (Numbers 9:8). Moses instructed the children of Israel to stand still. He needed to hear what the Lord was commanding them to do. Their movement would have caused Moses to miss what God wanted to say to them. Moses knew their inclination would lead them out of God's presence. Your flesh wants to lead you out of the presence of the Lord. It is not comfortable in his presence. No flesh can glory in his sight. Your flesh will want to avoid worship service. It will try to move you out of the place where God will speak to you. Your fleshly impulses will be against God. That is why it is so important for you to *stand still, and hear what the Lord will command concerning you.* Don't allow the distractions of the flesh to lead you out of the presence of the Lord. Adam's flesh (nakedness) lead him out of the presence of the Lord. God wanted to fellowship with him. He also wants to fellowship with you. Stand still and hear what the Lord is saying to you.

Quiet Storm

The Lord demonstrated himself mightily to the children of Israel. With a mighty hand, he led them out of Egypt. Now with the Red Sea in front and Pharaoh and his army at their backs, they needed to see his saving power again. God sent a windstorm to stir up the dust between Israel and their enemy. This was a great problem for the Egyptians, but a quiet comfort to the children of Israel. This <u>quiet storm</u> gave them the time they needed to cross over the Red Sea. When you are quiet and still before God, it seems as if everything else around you gets nosier. You hear the outside noise, the passing cars, sometimes even your own breathing. This may seem to be a distraction, but you should keep pushing. Like the eye of a storm, there is calmness in all that noise. At first it will seem strange but keep spending quiet time with God. It will become music to your ears. It will serve as an alarm that you are on your way to meet with God.

The eye of the storm represents the quiet place inside of your environment. When you become quiet everything around you comes alive. The clock, radio, TV, kids, neighbors, passing cars, and mental pictures all seem so loud. Noises you did not even notice before you decided to be quiet are loud and clear now. These noises are quiet distractions. Quiet distractions are things outside of your immediate control or sphere. You cannot turn off passing cars, or turn down the neighbors. These distractions will be there every time you decide to be quiet. You will have to learn how to press past these things. The Bible says study to be quiet. This means study how to press past distractions.

There is calmness in the mist of your distractions. Like the eye of the storm, it is calmness surrounded by chaos. The distractions are on the outside fringes of your consciousness. The calmness that you seek is at the center of your quietness. It is the attention and focus you place on God. *Thou (Lord God) wilt keep him in perfect peace, whose mind is stayed on thee: because he trusteth in thee (Isaiah 26:3)*. God should be at the center of your quietness. Adam's movement caused him to miss God. Don't move. Don't lose focus. *Be still, and know that I am God (Psalms 46:10)*. You are not just seeking to be quiet, you are seeking the face of God. Stillness helps you see the face of God.

Adam, Where Art Thou?

Adam hid himself, but God went looking for him. He was out of place and God knew it. God cried out to Adam "Where are you"? His desire was to commune with Adam. Adam's being out of place caused him to miss God. Adam hid because he was ashamed of his actions. Are you hiding from God? Are you out of place? When was the last time you quietly waited on God? He has so much he wants to tell you, and so much he wants to show you. Be still and know I am God. God will go to the place where he use to meet you. You should be there. He is the one that tells you when it's time to move on. Don't move without his leading. Get up in the morning and be still before God. Let him order your steps. Let him light your path. He is waiting for you in that place he use to meet you. You know that place. You use to lie on his shoulder there. He is there right now. Go to that place and sit quietly and commune with him. He is looking for you. Don't worry about explaining where you have been. You don't have to say a word. He has so much to share with you.

Try this little exercise. Find a quiet place. Sit down in a comfortable position and close your eyes. Hear all the noise? Don't worry you will learn to ignore it. Now, focus on the Lord. It may be a song, scripture or even a picture of the Lord that comes to your mind. Don't respond. Don't sing, speak, or hum, just listen. It may seem as though you are getting tired or sleepy, but you are not. Relaxation can bring on sleepiness, but it does not have to. Train your mind and body to pay attention to the still small voice of the Lord. Study to be quiet. Quietly wait on the Lord. He will meet you in that quiet place inside you. Don't worry about the time, God will let you know when it is time to move. There is a quiet place inside you reserved for God. I call this place the eye of the storm. There is quietness in the mist of chaos. *Let the words of my mouth, and <u>the meditation of my heart</u>, be acceptable in thy sight, O LORD, my strength, and my redeemer (Psalms 19:14).* It's your heart and not your mind that meditates on the Lord. He is your strength and your redeemer.

CHAPTER EIGHT

LOOSED,
BUT NOT CLEAN!

"HOW SHALL A MAN CLEANS HIS WAYS?"
PSALMS 119:9

Bob was in prison for 20 years for murdering a man. He had twenty years to reflect on his actions. During this time he received counseling and psychological evaluations. He seemed to have paid his debt to society. Years later, he was released from prison. A few days after being released, he turned himself into the police and confessed to murdering someone else. He was loosed from his prison but not from his torment. We are all free, but we are not all clean! In order for us to fully enjoy life we must be clean. Being quiet before the Father brings about a cleansing that is necessary to enjoy life.

The children of Israel were in captivity in Egypt for over four hundred years. They cried unto the Lord day and night for their deliverance. They were fed up with their present life. They desired a change. Sound familiar? With his mighty hand, God <u>loosed</u> them from their prison. They left the prison of Egypt only to be tormented by the same things. Lust, adultery, fear, and idolatry were not in the prison of Egypt but in the children of Israel. How sad it must have been for them. Getting loosed is only part of the solution. They needed to be cleansed as well. A person is not defiled by what goes into him but by what comes out of him. Fear came out of them. Lust came out of them. Adultery came out of them.

It is not enough for you to just get free. Have you been delivered in the past but are still hampered by the same things? Are you like the children of Israel battling with past sins? Do some of your ways still need cleansing? God wants to show you how to get clean and stay clean!

They are Your Ways

You are so excited about being free that you forget you need to be cleansed as well. God is not going to do it for you! How **shall a man** cleanse **his** ways! You have to cleanse your own ways! He has already created in you a clean heart. It is up to you to take the <u>provision </u>God has provided and cleanse your <u>own </u>ways!

*Know ye not that to whom ye yield **yourselves** servants to obey, his servants are ye to whom ye obey. (Romans 6:16)*

Are you yielding yourself? These ways are your ways. It is you that is doing the yielding and it is also you that must do the cleansing.

Even so now <u>yield your</u> members servants to right-eousness unto holiness (Roman 6: 19b). Yield means to give up possession of, to surrender, or relinquish to the physical control of another. When you yield yourself, you give someone or something control over you. This is your choice to make. Yielding to unclean things make you unclean. *Even so now <u>yield your</u> members servants to <u>right-</u>*

eousness unto *holiness* (*Roman 6: 19b*). Now you must learn how to yield yourself to serve righteousness and holiness. Don't worry, your Heavenly Father is waiting to help you. He will show you how to cleanse your ways.

How Shall A Man Cleanse His Ways?

How shall a man cleanse his ways? By taking heed thereto according to his word (Psalms 119:9). Listening to God and taking heed to his word will cleanse a man's ways. If you are too busy to listen, then you are too busy to be cleansed. It's up to you. When you heed the word you give attention or consideration to the word. You cannot become clean without the word of God. John 17:17 declares the truth of the word will sanctify you. This means the word of God will free you from sin. It is the word of God that you must use to free yourself from sin. Trying to cleanse your ways without the word of God is like washing with out soap. You will go though the motions, but you will not get the proper results. You need a cleaning solution to help you. The word of God is the solution. Giving heed to the word means you are allowing it to soak into your problem area. Some things have set in your heart and you need the word to break them up. Without the word of God you will never get clean. Bible study, Sunday school, and worship service are all a part of the solution process.

Let not sin therefore reign in your mortal body, that ye should obey unrighteousness unto sin; but yield yourselves unto God, as those that are alive from the dead, and your members as instruments of righteousness unto God. (Roman 6:12,13)

This process involves you. There are four references to "you" in the scripture. You are the one that keeps sin from reign in your body. <u>You</u> are the one who will not obey unrighteousness. <u>You</u> are the one who will yield <u>yourself</u> to God and your member (body) as righteous instruments to be used by him. What a revelation! What a unique concept! Let not sin reign in <u>your</u> body. You have a part to play in this process. If your mind is going to be renewed you have to let it! If your mind is going to be transformed you have to let it. You have the power to put yourself in the place, position and posture to be cleansed. God will do the part you can't, but you must do your part!

You are no stranger to doing your part. You take your children to the doctor. You place them in the emergency room, and then you let the doctor do the rest. You even take your car to the shop, place it on the lift, and then let the mechanic to do the rest. Why not take your mind, soul and spirit to God and let him do the rest? If you do your part God will do his. If you draw near to him he will draw near to you! God's process involves you. Learn to put yourself in the position, place and posture to be cleansed.

Lets look at what wonderful insight the bible gives to us on how to cleanse our ways.

The Word's Way to Cleansing

1. *How shall a man cleanse his ways? By taking heed thereto according to his word. (Psalms 119:9)*
Take heed to the word of God. Pay attention to the word of God. Don't let the word slip away from you. Take notes as often as you can. This will help increase your retention. It will also give you something to refer back to. Taking heed also means to put yourself in the position, place and posture to hear and understand the word of God. Ask questions if necessary. Remember to let God speak to you. Bible studies, Sunday school, worship services are all opportuni-

ties God uses to speak to you. Take <u>heed </u>thereto according to his word.

2. *Purge out the old leaven that ye may be a new lump. (1 Cor 5:7)*
A small amount of leaven works through the whole lump. Leaven is a substance that causes things to rise. It is those things that will cause situations, attitudes, egos, and blood pressure to rise. Leaven mixes so well into the lump that it is able to hide behind other things. First, you have to understand that the leaven is in you and not in other people. You have to get the leaven out of yourself. Second, leaven will rise under pressure. In any heated situation, leaven shows up. It causes a chemical reaction to take place. Leaven will split compounds. Leaven will divide relationships. Purge out the old. Get rid of that old leaven! Get rid of that old attitude! Go through your house and get rid of all those things that pertain to the old you. The Ephesians even went to the point of publicly burning their books of witchcraft. God is looking for you to do the purging. Make a list of the things you need to get rid of, and get rid of them!

3. *Let us cleanse our selves from all filthiness of the flesh and spirit. (2 Cor 7:1)*
Let us cleanse <u>ourselves</u>. Clean hands lead to a clean heart. When I was a little boy my mom always ensured I had on clean underwear. She knew clean underwear led to clean outerwear. To be clean on the outside, but filthy on the inside is not good. If you are clean on the inside the dust of life may land on you, but you will be okay. Clean heart leads to clean hands. Clean thoughts lead to clean actions. Clean underwear leads to clean outerwear. You must scrub your heart with God's word. Scrub out not being willing to forgive. This will defile you. The same measure you meet

will be measured back to you. You must forgive. *For if you do not forgive men their trespasses, neither will your father in heaven forgive your trespasses. (Mark 11:26)* Let us cleanse ourselves from the inside out.

4. *Submit yourselves therefore unto God. Resist the devil and he shall flee. (James 4:7)*
Submitting to God must proceed resisting the devil. You cannot resist the devil on your own; he is too crafty for you. He will only trick you into doing something against God. You must first submit to God. Submitting is an act of yielding oneself to the authority or will of another. You must be willing to give control over to God. Submitting does not involve force. God will not force you.

Allow your Heavenly Father to guide you around all the devil's traps and snares. There is no need to worry about what to do with the devil. Just submit to God and the devil will flee. God is waiting to tell you what to do in order to resist the devil. When you obey his instructions, you cause the devil to flee. Submit to God and resist the devil. God has put the ball in your court. Put yourself in the position to hear God's word. Faith comes by hearing, and hearing by the word of God. Submitting to God is resisting the devil.

5. *For not the hearers of the law are just before God, but the doers of the law shall be justified. (Romans 2:13)*
Webster defines the law as the will of God set forth in the Old Testament. So this scripture is referring to hearing and doing the will of God. Those that do the will of God are considered justified before him. Do the word. We have long prayer lines in our churches of people, who want prayer to be the answer to all their problems. They go from church to church, and conference to conference looking for help. Tired and weary from struggling with the same

problem, they often loose. There is no quick fix. Do the word! Nothing can substitute for time alone with God. Live the word! After you have heard the word, You must become a doer of the word. That is what will justify you.

Daily Cleansing

God says in his word to cleanse yourself, and your hands. He also says to submit yourself, yield your members, and purge out the old leaven. See the pattern. It's on you too. No more excuses. You are no longer yesterday's person. That person died yesterday. You have more information about yourself today than at any other time in your life. Tomorrow you will have even more! Each day a new you is born, new thoughts are created, and new actions are performed. Because of this, daily cleansing is necessary. *Let us cleanse ourselves 2Cor 7:1*. Being quiet before God is daily cleansing. During your quiet time with God you are free of thought, action, motion and communication. When you allow yourselves to become quiet, you can hear your breath, your heartbeat, and your God. In a still quiet voice God refreshes your soul, fills your mind, organizes your motions, and governs your actions. Chaos becomes calmness, words become actions, and breath becomes life. God aligns you with your environment and yourself. Study to be quiet is freeing your mind of your thoughts so God can fill it with his thoughts.

Let this mind be in you that was also in Christ Jesus (Phil. 2:5)
Jesus had the mind of the Father. As our example, he wants you to also have the mind of the Father. Jesus wants you to have the intention and desire that he and the Father have. You get the mind, intention, and desire of the Father by spending time with him and with Jesus (word).

Spending time with the Word, whether at home or at church, is only a part of it. You must spend time alone with the Father to know his mind. Jesus and the Father have the same mind and they are waiting to share it with you.

CHAPTER NINE

GOD HAS A PLAN FOR YOU

*"For I know the plans I have for **you**, plans to give **you** hope and a future. Then **you** will call upon me and come and pray to me, and I will listen to **you**. **You** will seek me and find me, when **you** seek me with all your heart. I will be found by **you**, declares the Lord. (Jeremiah. 29:11-14a)*

Peace with God brings about peace within yourself. Peace with yourself leads to knowledge of yourself. You begin to know the real you, the natural you. The word natural means, "of nature." Nature is the inherent character or the basic composition of a person or thing. Nature is the center of who you are. A bird flies naturally because it was designed to fly. A fish swims naturally because it was designed to swim. If you look at the things you do naturally, you can get a basic understanding of yourself.

True understanding can only be known in the mind of the creator. A bird was designed for more than just flying. It is a part of a greater plan. It is a part of the Eco-system you live in. It also has a purpose beyond the Eco-system. If you have questions of what the bird "can" and "should" do, you should ask the creator and not the bird. The bird only knows what it can do, it does not know "why" or "if" it should be doing it.

If you depend on your own knowledge, or rely on what you "can" do, you will always miss God! "His thoughts are not your thoughts, and his ways are not your ways" (Isaiah 55:8). Quiet reflection allows you to see yourselves as part of God's great plan. You become aware that you are more than a cog in the system. You are not here just to pass time away. You are here for more than what you can see or understand right now. God has a plan and a purpose for you.

You are a Part of God's Plan

Abram spent time with God and God showed him his plan for him. Abram was to be the father of all nations, even the father of faith. What a plan! Knowledge of God's plan changed Abram. His name changed. His environment changed. Self-awareness changes you to conform to God's plan for you. Once you discover God's plan for your life, all things become new. People treat you differently. Even God will treat you differently. God changed Abram's name to Abraham. God declared him to be blessed. If God says sometime about you, it is so. God blessed Abraham and now the people treated him differently as well. Abraham now had access to the king's court. He was now more than just another man living on earth. He was now a priest of the most high God! He was now a person able to bless nations!

You like Abraham are more than just another man or another woman. You are here for more than just working and paying bills. You are here to fulfill the intent of the creator. God wants to bless you and change your name. *He that hath an ear, let him hear what the Spirit saith unto the churches; To him that overcometh will I give to eat of the hidden manna, and will give him a white stone, and in the stone a new name written, which no man knoweth saving he that receiveth it (Revelation 2:17).* God has a wonderful new name reserved for you that is so precious and powerful, no one will know but you. He also wants to give you hidden manna to sustain you. God wants to give you what you need so others can be blessed through you. Nations need to be blessed through you. You are part of the Master's plan. You have a new name. You are now a Christian. You are now a child of God.

God's Plan Changes You

God's plan changes you. You cannot fulfill God's plan without changing. You must first become aware of who you are. Self-awareness leads to self-fulfillment. You cannot fulfill God's purpose for you if you do not know what he has planned for you. He has a plan for you, but you just can't see it right now. God does not reveal his plan to you all at once. You could not handle that. He intends for his plan to be time and event dated. There will be an event you your life that will trigger the plan God has for you. It may have been the day you were saved. It may have been the day you were filled with the Holy Spirit. Maybe it was the day you received your calling into ministry. For Abraham it was something much simpler. God told Abraham to leave the land of Ur. Abraham's "going out" triggered God's plan for him. This single event changed his life forever. He was now the called the father of faith and the father of many nations. He was no longer the same. His obedience to God changed who he was. This event was the beginning of a great nation. God's plan will change you and those around you.

It was not going to be easy for Abraham. He had a

lot of obstacles in his way, but it did not matter, God was going to do it for him. God's plan for you is not an easy plan. You must go through the wilderness to get to the promise land. Joseph had to go to the pit and the prison before he got to the palace.

God's Plan is not Easy

And they took him, and cast him into a pit: and the pit was empty, there was no water in it. Then there passed by Midianites merchantmen; and they drew and lifted up Joseph out of the pit, and sold Joseph to the Ishmeelites for twenty pieces of silver: and they brought Joseph into Egypt. And Reuben returned unto the pit; and, behold, Joseph was not in the pit; (Genesis 37:24,28-29).

The pit was a part of God's plan. If the plan that is before you is an easy plan, it is not God's plan. If you are in a pit right now, God has plans to bring you out. Your pit, your low point is an opportunity for God to bring you out. God's plan does not leave you in the pit.

God's plan is not easy. *And he said to them all, If any man will come after me, let him deny himself, and take up his cross daily, and follow me (Luke 9:23).* God's plan has a cross to bear. This cross cannot be taken up one day and put down the next day. It must be borne daily. There are some daily burdens you must shoulder. You cannot fulfill God's plan without a cross. His plan includes the cross. His plan includes mortifying the deeds of the body that seeks to kill you. *For if ye live after the flesh, ye shall die: but if ye through the Spirit do mortify the deeds of the body, ye shall live (Romans 8:13).* The easy plan will kill you. The easy plan includes living through the flesh. The easy plan satisfies the body, but it kills the spirit.

Just because a person is suffering does not mean they are in the plan of God. *But let none of you suffer as a murderer, or as a thief, or as an evildoer, or as a busybody in other men's matters. Yet if any man suffer as a Christian, let him not be ashamed; but let him glorify God on this behalf. Wherefore let them that suffer according to the will of God commit the keeping of their souls to him in well doing, as unto a faithful Creator (1Peter 4:15,16,19).* Not all suffering is according to the will of God. Suffering as a Christian is in God's plan. If you are suffering because of sin, you are not in God's plan. Joseph suffering the pit was not the result of sin. Moses suffering the wilderness was not the result of sin. Jesus suffering the cross was not the result of sin. God's cross for you to bear is not the result of sin.

If you are going through because of things you have done, you are not in the plan of God. Sin will hinder the plan God has for you. Repent, so God can forgive you and show you the real plan. *If we confess our sins, he is faithful and just to forgive us our sins, and to cleanse us from all unrighteousness (1 John 1:9).* God's plan includes forgiveness. His plan includes cleaning you from all unrighteousness. He is waiting to forgive you so he can show you the real plan he has for you.

God's Plan Takes Time

God's plan takes time. Abram was a hundred years old when his wife conceived his son Isaac. This was the time in his life when God chose to fulfill his promise to Abram. Time and events both have a part to play in God's plan. When you spend time with the Father, he will tell you when is the right time for you. You may feel like your season has passed, or that it is too late for you. Don't believe that. Abram was a hundred years old and God used him to become the father of many nations. You just need to be alone with God. He will encourage you. He will fulfill you. He will show you the wonderful things he has plan just for you.

"For I know the plans I have for __you__, plans to give __you__ hope and a future. Then __you__ will call upon me and come and pray to me, and I will listen to __you__. __You__ will seek me and find me, when __you__ seek me with all your heart. I will be found by __you__, declares the Lord. (Jer. 29:11-14a)

The real plan takes time. God has big plans for **you**! Plans to prosper you! Wow! That is awesome! The owner of all that is has plans to prosper you! Do you really know who you are? God's plans give you hope! Even if you don't have a future because of your past sins, he will give you one. When God spoke through Jeremiah, he was not talking to people who had done everything right. He was talking to the stiff-necked rebellious children of Israel. They had served other gods. They had forsaken the true and living God. God's response was "I have already made plans for you, and I have plans to prosper you!" Have you messed up in the past? God still has plans for you. If you seek him, you will find him. He has declared it. He will bring it too past.

Once you take the time to find out who you really are, you can find out the <u>real</u> plan the Father has for you. That other plan was not God's. That is the devil's plan for you. satan's plan is to kill you, to steal from you, and to distort God's plan for you. His plan is to lie to you about God's love for you. He is the one lying and saying because you did this or that, God does not love you anymore. He is trying to trick you into drugs, teenage pregnancy, crime, and all other kinds of "stuff." This is not the plan God has for you. God's plan is to show you the real you. He wants to show you the real plan for you. God's plan for you gives you hope and a future. His plan causes you to triumph over the enemy.

Now thanks be unto God which <u>always</u> causeth us to triumph in Christ (2Cor 2:14). You have a future, and your future is in Jesus! You are going to prosper and your prosperity is in Jesus! Spend time alone with the Father so he can show you who you really are. He wants you to fulfill his plan, his wonderful, prosperous plan that he has just for you. God always causes you to triumph. God always causes you to win. If you are not winning, you are not in the plan God has for you. He never planned for you to lose. He is waiting to show you how to win. *For I know the plans I have for <u>you</u>, plans to give <u>you</u> hope and a future. Then <u>you</u> will call upon me and come and pray to me, and I will listen to <u>you</u>. <u>You</u> will seek me and find me, when <u>you</u> seek me with all your heart. I will be found by <u>you</u>, declares the Lord. (Jer. 29:11-14a)*

God's Plan Requires Sacrifice

And he said, Take now thy son, thine only son Isaac, whom thou lovest, and get thee into the land of Moriah; and offer him there for a burnt offering upon one of the mountains which I will tell thee of (Genesis 22:2).

Abraham was instructed by God to offer his son Isaac as a sacrifice. Abraham only had one son and to give him up would have made him childless. How could he become the father of many nations if his only son was taken away? How was God going to complete what he had promised Abraham without Isaac? The list of questions about this situation could go on and on, but God's plan does not require questions. God's plan requires sacrifice. Sacrifice means you are offering something dear to you. Sacrifice defies understanding. It makes no sense to give when you don't have. It makes no sense to give your last. God is not asking you to make sense, he as asking you to make a sacrifice.

Abraham's only response was to obey God. He had no questions. Abraham was a man of action. Your sacrifice should compel you into action. It should be on your mind when you wake up in the morning. It should include everything necessary to make the sacrifice. When you prepare your sacrifice in advance, you show sincerity. You must be sincere when you give your tithes and offering. You should not forget your tithes and offering at home. Your sincerity to God should compel you to prepare it in advance and to bring it with you. *And Abraham rose up early in the morning, and saddled his ass, and took two of his young men with him, and Isaac his son, and clave the wood for the burnt offering, and rose up, and went unto the place of which God had told him. Then on the third day Abraham lifted up his eyes, and saw the place afar off (Genesis 22:3).*

Abraham sacrifice was more than just substance. Abraham sacrificed his time and himself. He got up early and began his journey. He had to travel for three days to get to the place God had instructed him to go. *Then on the third day Abraham lifted up his eyes, and saw the place afar off (Genesis 22:4).* Even after three days, the place where God wanted him was still afar off. He still had some more traveling to do. He was to give even more than he had already given. He was away from his family. He was between the comforts of home and the place God wanted him to be.

You have to leave home. You have to leave comfort. You have to leave family. You have to get up early in the morning and prepare. The place God has for you require sacrifice. You will not see it at first. You may have to travel a few days before you can see it. Just make sure you have everything with you. This will show God that you are sincere. There will be no time for you to go back and get anything. Your sacrifice begins with you. It begins when you decide to obey God. God's plan requires you to make a sacrifice.

God's Plan Requires Effort

God instructed Abraham to go to Mount Mariah. *And he said, Take now thy son, thine only son Isaac, whom thou lovest, and get thee into the land of Moriah; and offer him there for a burnt offering upon one of the mountains which I will tell thee of (Genesis 22:2).*

It took Abraham three days to get to the mountain. He had to carry all of the required items necessary to make the sacrifice. This was a tremendous effort. Now after all this, he was going to have to climb a mountain. He was going to have to climb it with some wood, some fire, a knife, and his son. He was going to have to climb it alone. What an effort! *Then on the third day Abraham lifted up his eyes, and saw the place afar off. And Abraham said unto his young men, Abide ye here with the ass; and I and the lad will go yonder and worship, and come again to you. And Abraham took the wood of the burnt offering, and laid it upon Isaac his son; and he took the fire in his hand, and a knife; and they went both of them together (Genesis 22:4-6).*

Once upon the mountain, Abraham still had to build an altar. He still had more work to do. He needed to finish what he started in order to fulfill the plan of God. You can not do part of the plan. You must do it all to be in the plan of God. There must be a sacrifice. Abraham never complained. He probably was heartbroken about having to offer his son. He probably was tired. He probably was hungry. But he had a job to do. He had a sacrifice to make. There is no excuse good enough not to obey God. God was the only one that could alter the plan. Abraham would have to just trust God. He just needed to do his part. He trusted God with his son. He knew God would provide.

*And Abraham said, My son, <u>God will **provide** himself a lamb</u> for a burnt offering: so they went both of them together. And* *they came to the place which God had told him of; and Abraham built an altar there, and laid the wood in order, and bound Isaac his son, and laid him on the altar upon the wood. And Abraham stretched forth his hand, and took the knife to slay his son. And the angel of the LORD called unto him out of heaven, and said, Abraham, Abraham: and he said, Here am I. And he said, Lay not thine hand upon the lad, neither do thou any thing unto him: for now I know that thou fearest God, seeing thou hast not withheld thy son, thine only son from me. And Abraham lifted up his eyes, and looked, and behold behind him a ram caught in a thicket by his horns: and Abraham went and took the ram, and offered him up for a burnt offering in the stead of his son. And Abraham called the name of that place Jehovahjireh: as it is said to this day, In the mount of the LORD it shall be seen (Genesis 22:8-14).*

God blesses your effort. Abraham gave up his son, and God gave him a nation. There is a benefit to obeying God. Your effort will be blessed. God will provide. He will give you blessing upon blessing. God plan includes multiplying what you have given. You must make the sacrifice. He cannot multiply it until you give it. Making the effort to give will cause your blessing to be multiplied. *And the angel of the LORD called unto Abraham out of heaven the second time, And said, By myself have I sworn, saith the LORD, for because <u>thou hast done this thing</u>, and <u>hast not withheld thy son</u>, thine only son: <u>That in blessing I will bless thee</u>, and in **multiplying** I will **multiply** thy seed as the stars of the heaven, and as the sand which is upon the sea shore; and thy seed shall possess the gate of his enemies; **And in thy seed shall all the nations of the earth be blessed; because thou hast obeyed my voice** (Genesis 22:15-18).*

Obeying God will cause you to be blessed. God will multiply the multiplying, and you will be blessed with a blessing because you have obeyed the voice of the Lord.

CHAPTER TEN

TODAY WILL BE A QUIET DAY

EXAMINE YOURSELVES, WHETHER YE BE IN THE FAITH; PROVE YOUR OWN SELVES. (2 COR 13:5)

"Today will be a quiet day." This is what you should say to start each morning. This simple declaration can help you understand the need for quiet time. Quiet time leads to self-examination. Self-examination is necessary. Check your condition on a daily basis. Check and see *whether ye be in the faith.* This requires you to check your previous actions to determine if they are in line with the plan God has for you. This is how you *prove your own selves.* You prove yourself by aligning yourself with the plan God has placed in your belly (spirit). "Today will be a quiet day," because I have taken the time to examine myself.

Self to Self Alignment

When I turn on my computer in the morning, it goes through a series of bleeps and flashes which it does every time it starts up. It checks to make sure all the drives and cylinders are operating correctly. It also checks the main memory to make sure none of the data has been corrupted since it was shut down on last night. It makes the minor adjustments necessary every morning to keep itself running smoothly. The computer checks itself against itself. These daily adjustments and alignments keep the computer from crashing. They are an essential part of the well being and longevity of the computer.

You are more complexed and complicated than a computer. If your home computer needs to align itself daily, how much more so do you need to check yourself? Many people skip this all-important function for a few extra minutes sleep in the morning. Important daily self-checks are not being performed. Because of this, your cylinders are skipping, your main memory is failing, and your system is headed for a crash. Systems crash when the hard drive becomes corrupted. Systems crash when memory fails. Daily adjustments in your life keep your hard drive running smoothly and yout memory from failing.

Spirit

Man is a very complicated system. He is a <u>spirit</u> that has a <u>soul</u> that lives in a <u>body</u>. That is why we refer to him as a triune man, three in one. His spirit is the total essence of who he is. He is a combination of what God has designed him to be, and what he has seen, heard, and done in the past. You have to be careful about what you see. The things seen and heard can corrupt the spirit of man. *And delivered <u>just Lot</u>, vexed with the <u>filthy conversation</u> of the wicked: (For that righteous man dwelling among them, in* *seeing and hearing, vexed his righteous soul from day to day with their unlawful deeds;) 2Pet.2: 7,8.* Lot was a just man, but what he saw vexed him. It vexed his righteous soul. Filthy conversations will vex you. Unlawful deeds will vex you. It will vex your spirit. It will vex your heart.

Spirit of a man is also referred in the Bible as the heart of man. It is from this large storage container that all that is good or bad in a man comes forth. Out of his heart (spirit) comes forth evil thoughts, adulteries, and all foolishness. The evil that is in the heart of a man will defile the man. It will corrupt him. "*And he said, that which cometh out of the man, that defileth the man. For from within, out of the heart of men, proceed evil thoughts, adulteries, fornication, murders, thefts, covetousness, wickedness, deceit, lasciviousness, and evil eye, blasphemy, pride, foolishness: All these evil things come from within, and defile the man (Mark 7: 20-23).*

If a man's spirit becomes corrupted he will murder, steal, deceive, and commit any other act his heart desires. Keeping his heart clean is one of man's biggest struggles. The heart is a big storage container. It is the place where man's desires are generated. If you continue to see and hear the wrong things, you will corrupt your heart. If you allow your heart to become corrupted, your desires will be corrupted as well. Keep your heart from being corrupted.

How do you keep your heart from being corrupted? That is a very good question. Your heart is a storage container that things proceed out of. To keep it from being corrupted you have to understand how storage containers work. All storage devices work off of the same basic design. They have two basic parts, the container and the gate.

Spiritual Container

The container is simple. It holds what has been placed in it. It does not care what is being stored as long as it will fit. The container will accommodate a variety of substances. It will hold the good as well as the bad, the spoiled as well as unspoiled and the seen as well as unseen. The container will make the adjustment necessary to accommodate more stuff. It will move out the unseen to make room for the seen. It can be adjustable. It can also be expandable.

Your heart is your spiritual container. It contains spiritual things. It holds things that cannot be seen. It holds the good and the bad. Your heart has the word of God in it. It also has evil things that proceed out of it. It has good things mixed in with bad things. Some things in your heart look good to you. You cannot operate on looks alone. You will be fooled by looks. It may be spoiled and sour. It may kill you if you taste of it. There are some things in your spiritual container that will kill you. They were ok when you first put them in, but now they have spoiled. Now they have gotten mixed in with other things, things that will kill you. In your heart is stuff that will kill you if you taste it. There are also some things in your heart that will kill you if you touch them. So don't rely on feelings either. One touch or taste could prove to be deadly. Since your heart is a spiritual container, it needs spiritual cleansing.

God is the only one that can cleanse out your heart. He is the only one that knows it. *The heart is deceitful above all things, and desperately wicked: <u>who can know it</u>? I the LORD search the heart, I try the reins, even to give every man according to his ways, and according to the fruit of his doings (Jeremiah 17:9,10).* Who can know it? God searches your heart and he evaluates your ways. He knows there are wicked things in your heart. He is the only one that can straighten it out. He will create a clean heart within you. He will renew a right spirit within you. *Create in me a clean heart, O God; and renew a right spirit within me (Psalms 51:10).* He will strengthen your heart if you wait on him. *Wait on the LORD: be of good courage, and he shall strengthen thine heart: wait, I say, on the LORD (Psalms 27:14).* He will cause your heart to rejoice. *The statutes of the LORD are right, rejoicing the heart (Psalms 19:8a).* God is the only one who should be allowed to clean out your spiritual container. Spend time with him. He will create a new heart within you.

God knows your heart and he will cleanse it up. He will not allow it to become corrupted. Spending time with God gives Him the opportunity to renew a right spirit within you. God will wash you and make you whiter than snow. Your spirit and your heart will be clean.

Spiritual Gate (Soul)

The gate is a door, fence, road, channel, window or opening that leads into your spiritual container. It is a means of entering and exiting your spiritual container. The <u>soul</u> of a man is his spiritual gate. It is where his <u>feelings</u>, <u>senses</u>, <u>thoughts</u>, <u>emotions</u>, and most importantly his <u>will</u> reside. The soul is fed thoughts, pictures, words, images, touches, from the senses. This information is processed and passed on to the <u>will</u>. The <u>will</u> of a man decides whether or not to pass the information on to his heart (spiritual container). If a man's soul is corrupted, he will pass all the bad things he has seen, heard, or felt, into his heart. His heart will act upon them.

Every day you need to check your soul against the good things of God that are in your heart. David said *"Thy word have I hid in mine heart, that I might not sin against thee" (Psalms 119:11).* Your soul needs to be checked daily to make sure it is in sync with the word of God. The good things in your heart are the words God has placed in your heart. The word in your heart will keep you from sinning.

It is the gate and not the container that controls what is allowed in the container. The soul is the entry way into the heart. The gate (soul) that is evil will allow evil things into the heart. Every thought that comes to you enters through one of your senses. When you allow your senses, feeling, touch, smelling, hearing, seeing, to govern your actions, you negate the word that is in your heart. You will behave just like a person who does not have the word at all. Your soul must be checked against the word in your heart. You must not be governed by your emotions. Even if you have been given a new heart, if your soul is not right, your heart will be corrupted again. The gate is the key. Your <u>will</u> is the gate. If your gate (will) is not under the control (authority) of God, it is just a matter of time before your heart becomes corrupted again.

The soul can only be changed by the word of God. Your <u>will</u> must become God's <u>will</u>, and your ways must become his ways. You cannot think differently without the word of God. Your thoughts are not his thoughts and your ways are not his ways (Isa 55:8). You need his word to think differently. As long as you think the same, you will act the same. If your actions are corrupted, it is because your thoughts are corrupted. Your <u>will</u> is not God's will. Every day your soul must be aligned, conformed, checked, and balanced to the word that is in your heart. *But if the Spirit of him that raised up Jesus from the dead <u>dwell in you</u>, he that raised up Christ from the dead shall quicken your mortal bodies by his Spirit that <u>dwelleth in you</u>." (Romans 8:11).*

Body

The third part of the triune man is the body. The spirit and the soul are housed in the body. The body is also referred to as the flesh. There is no good thing in the *flesh (Romans 7: 18)*. The flesh is contrary to the Spirit of God. As one person put it, "the flesh is a mess." They that are in the flesh cannot please God (Romans 8:8). It desires fleshly things *(Romans 8:5)*. It must be brought into subjection daily. If your flesh is allowed to go unchecked, your flesh will corrupt your soul and your soul will corrupt your heart.

To allow the flesh to go unchecked is spiritual suicide. The flesh can only do what the <u>will</u> of man allows it to do. It can desire things, but it is powerless to act without the consent of the <u>will</u>. Is your body acting up? Is it out of control? It is only doing what you have allowed it to do. I remember many times while I was out jogging, my flesh wanted to stop. It would send all kinds of signal to my brain on why I should stop, but my mind, my <u>will</u>, <u>made</u> it keep going! You have to <u>will</u> to do the things of God. Your body needs to be kept in constant check or it will get out of control. You need to mortify the deeds of the flesh. If you let your flesh control you, you will be led away from God! Quiet time with God will keep your body in subjection. Your body wants to sleep in. Getting up early to be alone with God keeps your body in check. It does not want to do it, but it has no choice but to get in line. Today will be a quiet day. Today I will allow God to keep my body in check.

Daily Examination

First Corinthians 11:28 says to let every man examine himself. Self-examinations is a private matter. You need time alone daily to check yourself out. Check out your physical body. Check it out in the natural and in the spiritual. It's OK to look yourself over in the mirror everyday but make sure you also check yourself out in God's mirror. Ask yourself, what kind of fruit did I bear on yesterday? Did I produce fruits of the flesh or fruits of the Spirit? Did my heart bring forth love or hate? Daily inventory keeps the junk from piling up in you. You must align yourself to the word within yourself. Self to self-alignment is a daily thing. Self-examination is a private thing between you and God.

Your self-examination must include God. The eastern religions have practiced the art of self-to-self examination for thousand of years. They practice daily to rid their minds of evil thoughts, which in turn, rids their body of evil actions. They have learned how to focus their internal energy even to the point of controlling their metabolic rate. I am not talking about self-to-self examination. I am talking about self-to-God examinations. I am talking about spending a little time alone every day with the Father to evaluate yourself.

"For if we would judge ourselves, we should not be judged. (1Cor 11:31). We have become so accustomed to someone else doing things for us. We want someone to pray for us, preach to us, motivate us, encourage us, and examine us! This will not do. You need to get involved with you! Encourage yourself! Judge yourself! Examine yourself! Remember you have a part to play in this. Quiet-time with God is not a ritual; it's a spiritual necessity. Sacrifice those 30 minutes in the morning. You are worth it. It will keep your spirit, soul and body in tune with God, and your will aligned with the word of God that is in your heart.

Thou wilt keep him in perfect peace, whose mind is stayed on thee: because he trusteth in thee. (Isaiah 26:3)

Self to God Alignment

When you practice checking youself against yourself, you leave God out your equation. You have essentially become a god unto yourself. Self-meditation, self-healing, and quantum leaping, is all a part of this movement. Don't get caught up in self-to-self-alignment. You will limit yourself. You will become limited to the human nature. You will only be able to think in terms of things that pertain to the realm of the soul. Your strength will become limited by the power of your mind. If your mind is weak and limited, you become weak and limited as well.

You cannot expand your soul without God. Your understanding is limited without God. You are negated to relying on your environment for help and support. You will become a worshiper of things. You are forced to worship the sun, the moon, the trees, and the waters. You will look to nature for help. Nature will become a god unto you, and you will worship nature and the things that come from nature. Wood, stone, clay, glass, gold, silver, and other precious stones will become gods as well. Without God in the equation, you ultimately will become a worshipper of yourself and the things around you. *"And changed the glory of the incorruptible God into an image made like to corruptible man, and to birds, and fourfooted beast, and creeping things. (Rom. 1:23)*

In the United States, we have become worshippers of money and the things money can bring. Movie stars, athletes, singers, drug dealers, cars, houses and anything that has or comes from money become gods unto us. *The love of money is the root of all evil.* Murder, killing, stealing are all by-products of worshipping the god of money. God is the balance to the equation. He keeps us centered on him, and on his word.

It's a Daily Personal Matter

Quiet time with God is a personal matter. It is done in a private place away from the crowd. Quiet time with God is man's way of saying, "I am not the creator of myself." By acknowledging God on a daily basis you give him reverence as the one you are allowing to order your steps. You reaffirm that you are not able, worthy, qualified, capable, equipped or wise enough to order your own steps. You give the Father permission daily to take control of your life. A thousand conferences and a million prayer lines cannot do this! This is a daily personal matter! There is no substitute.

I see the results of those who try to substitute time alone with the Father for a week long conference or an all night prayer session. They feel great for a while. Everything seems so clear right after the meeting. As time goes on, things become blurry. Focus becomes a problem. Steps become unclear and direction becomes unsure. The further they get away from the meeting the worse it gets. They need.... Another conference, another prayer meeting, another quick fix! You can become addicted to prayer lines, meetings, seminars, conferences and the likes there of!

If your conference time is greater than your quiet time, you are out of balance. If your worship time is greater than your quiet time you are out of balance. What a mistake it is to think you can substitute daily time alone with the Father for a week long meeting or a shut-in at church. Now I am not saying not to attend. They have their place. I am saying no more using them as a substitute for time alone with God. The conference and the shut-in should be in addition your private time with God. There are some things in you that only time alone with God can fix. There are some areas in your heart that only time with God can reach. Your private worship must supercede your public worship. This will get you the answers that you need.

It's In God

If there is an answer to your problem, it's in God. Align yourself with him. Let his directions become your directions. Let his plan become your plan. Your salvation is in God. Your peace is in God. Even your riches are in God. *"But thou shalt remember the LORD thy God: for it is he that giveth thee power to get wealth, (Deu 8:18).* The children of Israel went to God daily because of their evil taskmasters. The problem was they went crying, complaining, weeping, and wailing. You need not follow this example. When you go to the Father, you need to go listening. Can you see him as the solution to your problem? If so why not let him solve it. I am not talking about the microwave quick fix you are accustomed to. I am talking about giving God the green light to work on your problems. I am talking about God cleaning out years of hurt, bitterness, loneliness, regrets, and anger. Let Him work on habits that have cemented themselves to your spirit, soul, and body.

You need daily time with God. You see, the remedies for your problems are in God! *"Seek the Lord while he may be found, call upon him while he is near. And let the wicked man forsake his way, and the unrighteous may his thought"* (Isaiah 55:6,7). Forsake your way for God's way and your thoughts for God's thought. Get in God and he will get in you. *"Draw nigh unto God and he will draw nigh unto you." James 4:8.* It's in God!

Today will be a quiet day. I will not trade time alone with the father for a few extra minutes sleep. That extra sleep will not do more for me than time alone with the Father. Time with the Father will refresh me. I will get up thirty minutes early to be with God. I will start each morning with the study of being quiet. I will quiet my mind so my heavenly Father can quiet my spirit, soul, and body. This is my affirmation I make to myself. I will be true to myself from this day forward. I present my spirit, soul, and body to my Heavenly Father so he can align it with his word. Because of this, today will be a quiet day.

CHAPTER ELEVEN

BLESSED, BROKEN, AND USED

Spiritual Environment

"For Moses had said, Consecrate yourselves today to the LORD, even every man upon his son, and upon his brother; that he may bestow upon you a blessing this day." (Exodus 32:29)

Before God used the children of Israel, he had to consecrate their spiritual environment. The children of Israel were instructed to drive out the inhabitants of the land that they were to posses. God knew the children of Israel would collect "stuff" along the way. He was calling them out of Egypt into the wilderness, so he could consecrate them. There, he would teach them his laws and statutes. Their new spiritual environment would be instrumental in them being blessed. This would be the first step to a new relationship with God.

Israel's time alone with God in the wilderness was filled with miracles, blessings, wonder and amazement. Their clothes never wore out, nor did their feet out grow their shoes. Although there were no animals for meat or clothing, God did not allow a single one to go naked or hungry. The exact amount of manna and quail was measured out on a daily basis. God caused water to flow out of a rock, the sun to stand still for a day, giants to fall, kingdoms to be conquered, a sea and river to part, and enemies to be destroyed. All of these great things took place in the <u>wilderness,</u> and not on the mountaintop! Remember to choose a spiritual attitude that will humble you and not exalt you before God.

There are blessings in your wilderness. Are you going through a wilderness experience? Don't worry, God is just cleaning up your spiritual environment. He is going to work some great wonders and miracles in your life just like he did for the children of Israel. Get ready! God wants to reveal his glory through you. *For I reckon that the sufferings of this present time are not worthy to be compared with the glory which shall be revealed in us (Romans 8:8).* Your present environment is temporary. The glory to be revealed is greater than your present suffering. You are going to be blessed. You are on your way to the promise land.

God has a work He is performing in you. He is creating a new spiritual environment within you. It is a three-fold process. A pastor friend of mine shared an illustration of this. He told me to examine the communion process. Christ took the bread, blessed it, broke it, and then used it. God first blesses you, then he breaks you of your will and your ways, and then he uses you.

Remember when you first got saved? God answered your entire prayer request instantly. Everything went your way. You wondered why you waited to get saved because everything was so blessed. If God did not bless you first you would have ran back to the world in a hurry. He had to strengthen you so you would be able to withstand being broken. He has a work he is performing in you. In-between God blessing you and using you is God breaking you. You must be broken. It is part of the process.

Time of Blessing

The wilderness is a part of Israel's spiritual environment. The wilderness was Israel's time of blessing. They did not work, cook, clean, shop, wash, farm, or any other thing they normally would have been required to do. God took on that responsibility for them. Hallelujah! What a blessing to be delivered from that evil taskmaster (daily chorus, bills, etc.). How many of us are in a position where we don't have to do anything? Would you consider it a blessing to be able to just worship and hear from God?

I suggest to you that every morning when you get up, you can create such an environment! Maybe you can't do it for 40 years like the children of Israel, but you can do it for 40 minutes. You can have 40 minutes of no working, cooking, cleaning, just you and the Father alone. This quiet separated time is your wilderness! This is your time of blessing and miracles! The Promise Land was not that promising anyway! They had to cross a sea to get there. They had to fight their way in. Evil kings ruled over them, and their enemies constantly besieged them. They had to work, cook, clean, farm, fight, and worship all at the same time. The book of the Law was lost, idol gods were found, and prophets were slain. Your real promise land is your time alone with God. Your environment of humility is your environment of blessing. Go fellowship with God, and enjoy your promise land.

Time of Breaking

The children of Israel needed to be spiritually broken. They were spiritually spoiled. The very things God had blessed them with, gold and silver, were the very things they began to worship.

And when the people saw that Moses delayed to come down out of the mount, the people gathered themselves together unto Aaron, and said unto him, Up, make us gods, which shall go before us; for as for this Moses, the man that brought us up out of the land of Egypt, we wot not what is become of him. And Aaron said unto them, Break off the golden earrings, which are in the ears of your wives, of your sons, and of your daughters, and bring them unto me. And all the people brake off the golden earrings which were in their ears, and brought them unto Aaron. And he received them at their hand, and fashioned it with a graving tool, after he had made it a molten calf: and they said, These be thy gods, O Israel, which brought thee up out of the land of Egypt (Exodus 32:1-4).

They changed the image of God into something corruptible, something made with hands. *Who changed the truth of God into a lie, and worshipped and served the creature more than the Creator, who is blessed forever. Amen (Romans 1:25).* Anytime you begin to worship the creature more than you worship the creator; you need to be broken spiritually.

God does the breaking; he knows what it takes to break you of your "stuff." It took 70 years in Babylon to <u>break</u> the children of Israel of their idol worship. They spent 70 years in exile, 70 years in time-out. Though it may have been painful, it was necessary. It worked. There is no record in the Bible of them worshiping idols after their 70 years in Babylon. God broke them of their idol worshipping. Now, he was able to use them. You have to be broken before you can be used. Don't allow the things he has given you to become the very things you worship.

You have to be broken spiritually before you can be used. That's just the way it is. Your "stuff" will get in the way. God has to take the necessary steps to rid you of your stuff. If necessary, there is a Babylon experience waiting on you. Make it easy on yourself. Get rid of the "stuff" that will keep you from being used by God. You will not regret it.

Time to Be Used

God did not break the children of Israel just to break them. He had plans of using them. He wanted them to be the ones that entered into the promise land. He wanted them to be the ones that built the temple. They would be the loins He would use to bring forth the Messiah. They were broken to be used.

God wants to use you. He has some spiritual things he wants you to do. He is breaking you so he can use you. You are not going through the <u>fire</u> just to be going through. God wants to save you. *If any man's work shall be burned, he shall suffer loss: but he himself shall be saved; yet so as by fire (1Cor 3:15).* He is taking you to a place in him that will allow you to fulfill his plan. It may seem like you are going around in circles, but you are not. God is holding you where you now to cleanse you of something. Some of your things cannot go into the promise land. Some of your ways cannot go into the promise land. Get rid of your ways so you can move into the place where God wants you to be. Then and only then will God be able to use you to lead others away from idol gods to the true and living God! Your wilderness is your blessing. Your time with God is your blessing. Create your wilderness today. God is consecrating your spiritual environment. Get alone with the father and let him bless you.

Natural Environment

Which the LORD commanded Moses in mount Sinai, in the day that he commanded the children of Israel to offer their oblations unto the LORD, in the wilderness of Sinai (Lev 7:38).

After God finishes with your spiritual environment, he wants to deal with your natural environment. Your natural environment is very important. What you see, smell, taste, touch, and hear will affect your spirit. Being in the wrong place at the wrong time can have disastrous results.

"And it came to pass, after the year was expired, at the <u>time when kings go forth to battle</u>, that David sent Joab, and his servants with him, and all Israel; and they destroyed the children of Ammon, and besieged Rabbah. But <u>David tarried still at Jerusalem. And it came to pass in an eveningtide, that David arose from off his bed, and walked upon the roof of the king's house: <u>and from the roof he saw a woman washing herself; and the woman was very beautiful to look upon</u>" (2Kg 11:1,2).</u>

David was out of place. He was supposed to be at war. He was a warrior. His place was leading the men of Israel into battle. Because of his success he became bored. He was not supposed to be on the roof. He was out of the place God had intended him to be. From the rooftop, David was able to see the kingdom. He was able to see Bathsheba. Seeing her caused him to want her. He did not want her before he saw her.

Some people would say, "It doesn't hurt to look." David was just looking. From this seemingly harmless act, adultery was committed, a man was killed, a child died, and a kingdom was humbled. When we put ourselves in place to see things, we put ourselves in place to lust after them. *"For all that is in the world, the lust of the flesh, and the lust of the eyes, and the pride of life, is not of the Father, but is of the world" (1John 2:16).*

Your natural environment involves what you see, if you see it you will want it. This is no mystery. The commercial world banks on this! They know if you see it long enough you will want it! Everything you see in advertisements is to make you want what you see. David was a man after God's own heart, but he was no different. David saw Bathsheba and he had to have her. This could have been avoided if he was in the right place. If his environment was right, he would have never have seen her. He never would have desired her. His lust for Bathsheba was a by-product of him being out of place. What problems has being out of place caused you? What situations could you have avoided? What disaster could you have prevented? Your natural environment is very important to maintaining a right relationship with God.

Your natural environment should be surrounded with Godly things. The environment you choose to be still and quiet before God is very important. If your natural environment is surrounded with things of the world that you can see, hear, smell, touch or feel it will only distract you away from God. The smell of bacon frying, sound of your favorite song, and sight of the morning news show can all remove you from that quiet place with God. These seemingly harmless acts can become compounded into long term problems with negative outcomes. What you perceive with your senses can work for you or against you. If you surround yourself with the things of God, you will want or desire the things of God. It works both ways.

Try this. Pick a place that is quiet and free from

movement or distractions. Choose sounds that will aid in creating an environment conducive to fellowshipping with God. Remove anything that is causing you to be distracted. This may take some trial and error, or even require some adjustment to your living arrangement, but it is too important for you to let that stop you. God has ordained a special place for you and him to meet. Seek him on where that place is.

And they heard the voice of the LORD God walking in the garden in the cool of the day: and Adam and his wife hid themselves from the presence of the LORD God amongst the trees of the garden.

Spiritual Position

*And Jesus entered and passed through Jericho. And, behold, there was a man named Zacchaeus, which was the chief among the publicans, and he was rich. And he sought to see Jesus who he was; and could not for the press, because he was little of stature. And he ran before, and <u>climbed up into a sycamore tree to see him</u>: for he was to pass that way. And when Jesus came to the place, he looked up, and saw him, and said unto him, Zacchaeus, **<u>make haste, and come down</u>**; for to day I must abide at thy house (Luke 19:1-5).*

Zacchaeus wanted to see Jesus. Because of the crowd and his shortness in stature he was not able to. So he picked a place in the path where Jesus was to pass by and climbed a tree. This was a bold move for Zacchaeus. To put oneself in the place to see Jesus would ensure him of being in the right place at the right time. Jesus arrived at the spot where Zacchaeus had climbed the tree and ordered him to come down at once. You see Zacchaeus was in the right place, but the wrong spiritual position! He positioned himself spiritually in a place where Jesus had to look up to him. Zacchaeus did it for a good reason and had no self glory in mind when he did it. His intentions were probably good, but he was still in the wrong position spiritually.

What is your spiritual position as it relates to Jesus? Are your desires for yourself greater than your desire to see Jesus? If so you must reposition yourself. You must reposition your desires. When it comes to Jesus, you must take a position of humility. You cannot exalt your desires, will, emotions, possessions, or relationships above that of Jesus. Jesus must be glorified. He must be exalted. You must humble yourself before the Lord God almighty! You position spiritually must be you looking up to God, and not God looking up to you. Like Zacchaeus, you must come down at once.

Natural Position

The natural environment of being quiet is more than just place or position. There are other personal aspects to be considered. If you are tense, upset, hurried, tired, hungry, or in pain it will ultimately affect the way you interact with God. None of these things will of themselves prevent you from getting through to God, but they will require much more discipline, concentration, and commitment than if they did not exist. The way you come to God will be the combination of your natural environment, spiritual disposition, and overall physical well being. I came up with this easy to remember acronym to help with this process. BRASS is a five-word phrase that will help you remember what you should be doing. It is the acronym used in the Marines to help a person focus in on the target during rifle training. Weather, posture, position, and pain all have to be overcome if one is to hit the target. Each letter applies to a principle you must learn.

B **reath**- focus on God, life is in the breath: your breath comes from God.

R **elax**- relax your body, get in a position that is comfortable. Be still.

A **im**- aim your focus upward; desire things from above not beneath.

S **ilence**- no talking, what God has to say is too important to miss.

S **olitude**- no television, no radio, no friends, just you and the Father.

Natural Man Holy God

God is nigh unto them of a humble heart and contrite spirit, but rest assured, he longs to fellowship with you. He has a time and a place appointed to meet you. You are natural; he is spiritual. Take off your shoes for you are standing on holy ground! It is the presence of God that sanctifies any person, building, church, mountain, valley, place or thing.

God will not meet with you because you are holy. He will meet with you because he is Holy and you are his child. As a father, he longs to fellowship with his children! You create an environment that is pleasing unto God, and he will show up. *"But thou art holy, O thou that inhabitest the praises of Israel"(Psalms 22:3).* He will come into your praise and abide in your worship. *"Be still and know I am God"(Psalms 46:10).* Go now and look for a place to fellowship with God. Make sure there are no distractions. Make sure you will be comfortable as you wait patiently on him. He will come! Your father always keeps his word and his appointments. Remember that you are natural, but he is spiritual.

CHAPTER TWELVE

QUIETLY BLESSED

"AND MOSES WAS AN HUNDRED AND
TWENTY YEARS OLD WHEN HE DIED:
HIS EYE WAS NOT DIM, NOR HIS NATURAL
FORCE ABATED." (DEUT. 34:7)

Natural Abilities

Moses was an ordinary man like most of us. He was a
Hebrew raised in Pharaoh's house. He murdered a man
and found himself on the run. He had low self-esteem and
considered himself a poor speaker. He argued with God
until God sent his brother Aaron to speak for him. After
spending time alone with God, he became a mighty man,
a man of greatness. He led the children of Israel out of
Egypt after 400 years of bondage. God performed mighty
miracles through him. His greatness was not because of any
deeds performed, but was a direct result of time he spent
with the Father. His confidence was multiplied, his words
were sure, difficult became easy, and impossible became

possible. Had he not spent time alone with God, he would have been just another stubborn, rebellious, stiff-necked, Israelite. Moses was great because he spent time alone with God.

God blessed Moses. He was a hundred and twenty years old when he died, and he was still able to see and all his natural abilities were in tact. Natural ability usually diminishes over time, but Moses had all of his. He could see and hear. He could still produce children. *"And Moses was an hundred and twenty years old when he died: his eye was not dim, <u>nor his natural force abated</u>" (Deut. 34:7).*

Like Moses, you need time with God. Church alone cannot do this for you. You need to spend time <u>alone</u> with God. Remember private worship plus public worship equals your total worship. You need them both. Spend time with the Father, and watch your confidence, courage, commitment, dependability, endurance, peace, joy, love and all your resources increase.

Time alone with God prolongs your natural strength. While others are stumbling and falling, you are still running. They will become naturally weary, but you will not. You are still able to dance in the Lord.

He giveth power to the faint; and to them that have no might he increaseth strength. Even the youths shall faint and be weary, and the young men shall utterly fall: <u>But they that wait upon the LORD</u> shall renew their strength; they shall mount up with wings as eagles; they shall run, and not be weary; and they shall walk, and not faint (Isaiah 40:29-31.)

Moses was a natural man, like you and me. He was not great on his own. God made him great. God wants to make you great. He wants to keep you from falling. *Now unto him that is able to <u>keep you from falling</u>, and to present you faultless before the presence of his glory with exceeding joy, (Jude 1:24).* He will present you faultless before his presence with exceeding joy. God is joyous about being with you. He is the only wise God that is able to keep you. *To the only wise God our Saviour, be glory and majesty, dominion and power, both now and ever. Amen (Jude 1:25).*

Natural Blessing

Now the LORD had said unto Abram, Get thee out of thy country, and from thy kindred, and from thy father's house, unto a land that I will shew thee: And I will make of thee a great nation, and I will <u>bless</u> thee, and make thy name great; and thou shalt be a <u>blessing</u>: And I will <u>bless</u> them that <u>bless</u> thee, and curse him that curseth thee: and in thee shall all families of the earth be <u>blessed</u> (Genesis 12:1-3).

Abram left his kinsmen in Haran at the request of God to spend time alone with him. He left all his luxuries at home to live the life of a nomad, but Abram was blessed, very blessed. God promised to bless him, and to make him a blessing. If God blesses, you are blessed. You have nothing to worry about. *"God is not a man, that he should lie; neither the son of man, that he should repent: hath he said, and shall he not do it? or hath he spoken, and shall he not make it good?," (Numbers 23:19).* God promised to bless. He will make it good. Moses left Haran. He was alone with God, and God blessed him because of it.

Maybe you feel like quiet time alone with God will take time away from your family, or from your ability to work and make money. It will not. It will only cause you to be blessed. God blesses you with wisdom and knowledge that will enable you to be abundantly blessed. *But thou shalt remember the Lord thy God: <u>for it is he</u> that giveth thee power to get wealth"(Duet. 8:18).* Time alone with God will result in you being blessed. *"Delight yourself in me and I will give you the desires of your heart"(Ps. 37:4).*

And Abraham was old, and well stricken in age: and the LORD had blessed Abraham in <u>all things</u> (Genesis 24:1). God blessed Abraham in all things. There was not an area in his life that he was not blessed in. *And Abram was very rich in cattle, in silver, and in gold (Genesis 13:2).* He was blessed in the city and in the field. *Blessed shalt thou be in the city, and blessed shalt thou be in the field (Deuteronomy 28:3).* He was blessed with cattle and sheep, and menservants and womenservants. *And Abimelech took sheep, and oxen, and menservants, and womenservants, and gave them unto Abraham, and restored him Sarah his wife.* Abraham was not blessed on his own. It was the Lord that blessed him. *And the LORD hath blessed my master greatly; and he is become great: and he hath given him flocks, and herds, and silver, and gold, and menservants, and maidservants, and camels, and asses (Genesis 24:35).* God made good on his promise to bless him. Time alone with God caused him to be naturally blessed.

God wants to bless you like he blessed Abraham. He wants to bless you in the city and in the field. He wants you to be rich. He has made you a promise as well. *For the LORD God is a sun and shield: the LORD will give grace and glory: <u>no good thing will he withhold from them that walk uprightly</u> (Psalms 84:11).* He will not withhold any good thing from you if you will allow him to show you how to walk upright. He wants you to have the desires of your heart. *Delight thyself also in the LORD: and he <u>shall give thee the desires of thine heart</u> (Psalms 37:4).* He wants to give you the kingdom. *Fear not, little flock; for it is your Father's good pleasure to give you the kingdom (Luke 12:32).* God wants to bless you with natural things. He wants to bless you like he did Abraham. Leave your family, friends, and love ones for a while to spend time alone with your Father. You will be glad you did.

Spiritual Benefits

There are spiritual benefits to being still before God. When you give him control of your life on a daily basis, the stress of what to do is removed. He gives you his peace. You have the creator of the whole universe ordering your footsteps. God removes the worry out of daily living. You are not stressed out because you know that God is guiding you, and he will not lead you astray. The peace of God adds additional years to your life. You become happier and more productive. *"Thou shall keep him in perfect peace who mind is stayed on him"(Isa. 26:3)*.

He also increases your strength. *"It is God that girdeth me with strength"(Ps. 18:32)*. He lightens your burdens and carries your load. *"Come unto me all ye that labor and are heavy laden, and I will give you rest"(Matt. 11:28)*. God has given you so many reasons to fellowship with him. He has so much to share with you, and he has so much he wants to do for you.

God will spiritually multiply your substance. Those that stayed in Jesus presence were fed in the wilderness. He will multiply what you already have to bless you. *And when evening had come, the disciples came to him, saying, This place is <u>waste land</u>, and the time is now past; send the people away so that they may go into the towns and get themselves food. But Jesus said to them, There is no need for them to go away; give them food yourselves. And they say to him, We have here but five cakes of bread and two fishes. <u>And he said, Give them to me</u>. And he gave orders for the people to be seated on the grass; and he took the five cakes of bread and the two fishes and, looking up to heaven, <u>he said words of blessing</u>, and made division of the food, and gave it to the disciples, and the disciples gave it to the people. And they all took of the food and had enough: and they <u>took up twelve baskets full of broken bits which were not used</u>. And those who had food were about five* *thousand men, in addition to women and children (Matthew14:19-21).* You can be blessed by being in God's presence. He will spiritually multiply whatever you bring to him. Being in God's presence will heal you spiritually. You will not have to go to the doctor. You will not have a medical bill. God himself will heal you. *And Jesus went about all the cities and villages, teaching in their synagogues, and preaching the gospel of the kingdom, and <u>healing every sickness and every disease among the people</u> (Matthew 9:35).*

God Will Satisfy Your Natural Desires

Time alone with God will satisfy your natural desires. Moses spent 40 days with God on the mountain and never got hungry. He did not eat for 40 days! Being alone in the presence of God satisfied his natural desires. Although, he went forty days without food, God satisfied his spirit, and his natural desires had to get in line. Get in line means to have control over. When you have control over your desire to eat, you have control over all your other desires. Hunger, lust, pride, sleep, anger and their likes will have to get in line. Is your body out of control? Spend some time with the Father! Is your mind going crazy? Spend some time with the Father! Your desires will get in line! They have to. *"That no flesh shall glory in his presence"(1Cor. 1:29).* Your "stuff" will be with you as long as you are not with him! Take heed to the word of God and cleanse your ways. Your natural desires are satisfied when you are with God.

Moses' fast for forty days without natural food was only possible, because he was <u>alone</u> with the father. If he had tried to go up on a mountain alone to fast for forty days, he would have died. You cannot live on bread alone. You need the word of God to live in the absence of bread. *But he answered and said, It is written, Man shall not live by bread alone, but by every word that proceedeth out of the mouth of God (Matthew 4:4).* You are not alone. If you go on a fast, take the Lord with you. Take the word of God with you. Your natural abilities will not sustain you. You need every word that proceeds out of the mouth of God.

God has spiritual meat for you. Jesus told his disciples his meat was to do the will of his father and to finish his work. *Jesus saith unto them, My meat is to do the will of him that sent me, and to finish his work (John 4:34).* The will of the Father was Jesus' spiritual meat.

You are blessed spiritually when you are with God. He has ordained it to be so. Every moment you spend with him is a blessed moment. He will bless your spirit, soul and body. *And the very God of peace sanctify you wholly; and I pray God your whole spirit and soul and body be preserved blameless unto the coming of our Lord Jesus Christ (1 Thessalonians 5:23).* He will keep you blameless and present you faultless. *Now unto him that is able to keep you from falling, and to present you faultless before the presence of his glory with exceeding joy (Jude 1:24).* Study to be quiet is the study of being blessed.

Write it Down

Keep a journal. Write down what God tells you during your quiet time with him. Write the date, time, and what God speaks into your spirit. This is very important. You cannot remember everything. Writing things down frees your mind to think on new things. This keeps your thoughts clear. Write down the good things that he has to share with you. You will be writing the plan God has for you a little at a time. *But the word of the LORD was unto them precept upon precept, precept upon precept; line upon line, line upon line; here a little, and there a little (Isaiah 28:13a).* God is blessing you with blessing on top of blessing. He has so much he wants to share with you. *And the LORD answered me, and said, Write the vision, and make it plain upon tables, that he may run that readeth it (Habakkuk 2:2).*

Thirty Day Test

There are some obvious benefits to being quiet. When we are still before God we find our lives a lot simpler. This is a simple truth. Most of our problems are due to the fact we do not spend enough time with God. The children of Israel benefited from time alone with God. They won battles, overcame adversities, and saw great miracles. Time with God allows you to see miracles. It's on you now. You have read the book, now what? Reading this book is a good start, but you need some practical application. Lets began today by implementing the plan. Get up thirty minutes earlier and "study to be quiet. I give you my word; your life will be better. Take the test. *"Let God be true and every man a liar"(Romans 3:4).* You will see the benefits, because God has already blessed you. Follow these simple steps.

1. Find a quiet place.
2. Create the right environment.
3. Get in a comfortable position.
4. Remember the acronym BRASS.
5. Keep a prayer journal
6. Write down daily what the Father says to you.
7. Watch God work!

Conclusion of the Whole Matter

"Let us hear the conclusion of the whole matter: Fear God, and keep his commandments: for this is the whole duty of man." *(Eccl 12:13).* You cannot live without God. The

whole duty of man is to fear God and keep his commandments. Time away from God is the beginning of death. The
children of Israel saw many people die in the wilderness.
Families were swallowed up in the earth, killed by plagues,
and stoned to death. When you separate from God you
begin to die. Your sins can and will separate you from God.
*But your iniquities have separated between you and your God,
and your sins have hid his face from you, that he will not hear
(Isaiah 59:2).*

Being still before God does not supersede the fact
you need a Savior. You need to include Jesus in your life.
Without him, you like many of them that left out of Egypt
will die in the wilderness. No blessing can freely flow
through you without you being free. *If the Son therefore
shall make you free, ye shall be free indeed (John 8:36).*
Salvation is man's way of saying "Okay God, I am ready for
you to instruct me, and for you to make me free."

*"But the natural man Receiveth not the things of the
Spirit of God: for they are foolishness unto him, neither can
he know them, because they are spiritually discerned"(1Cor.
2:14).* You will never obtain peace without God. Trying to
achieve inner peace through prayer, fellowship and meditation without Jesus is like putting gas in a car that has no
engine. It looks good, but it will get you nowhere. If you
will confess with your mouth the Lord Jesus, and believe
in your heart God has raised him from the dead you shall
be saved! Confess Jesus today and receive the peace of God
that passes all understanding. *Marvel not that I said unto
thee, Ye must be born again (John 3:7).* Study to be quiet
and be blessed.

ABOUT THE AUTHOR

Timothy L. Houston was born in Saginaw, Michigan to the late J. T. Houston and Levater Houston (Hughes). He received his early Christian training at Coleman Temple C.O.G.I.C. in Saginaw, Michigan. He is currently an associate elder at Greater Grace Church of God in Christ in Albany, Georgia. He has participated in ministries throughout the USA, and also in Japan and Korea. He is the former pastor of Acts Tabernacle Christian Center in Okinawa, Japan; and Word of Victory Church of God in Christ in Albany, Georgia. He is a motivational speaker and professional writer. A thirteen year Marine veteran, Elder Houston and his wife Linda, and children, Anetra, Tinesha, Nicole, Tim Jr., and Tamia reside in Albany, Georgia. Jesus Christ is the center of their lives.